WARRIOR NOTES HOMESCHOOLING

Bible Book 2
2nd Grade
Units 4-6

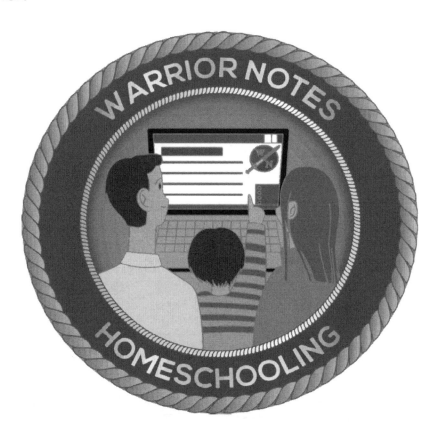

Warrior Notes Homeschooling

2nd grade Curriculum: Bible book 2

A concise and balanced curriculum that will help build a solid foundation in Bible with God's love at the forefront.

1 John 4:19 TPT
"Our love for others is our grateful response to the love God first demonstrated to us."

1 Corinthians 13:2 TPT
"And if I were to have the gift of prophecy with a profound understanding of God's hidden secrets, and if I possessed unending supernatural knowledge, and if I had the greatest gift of faith that could move mountains, but have never learned to love, then I am nothing."

Table of Content

Warrior Notes Homeschooling
Second Grade Bible

Focus: Value and Identity

Before every lesson, each child should pray a prayer so that their heart is ready to receive the Word of God. We have provided a prayer for you to use, but you can use your own prayer if you like: "Lord God, prepare my heart so that it has fertile soil for the Word of God to fall on, so that it will produce fruit in my life. Open my ears to hear Your Word, and open my eyes to understand Your Word. In Jesus name, amen."

Every week has a new Bible verse, and the students are encouraged to memorize the verse of the week. Learning to memorize scriptures is a powerful way for young children to learn the Bible. Students will fill in the blank with the correct missing weekly scripture verse.

Students will also be asked to learn at least one important thing from the week's lessons and tell you about it, write it down, and/or draw a picture about it for the weekly assessment.

Each lesson has an opening prayer, the Bible memory verse, The Bible lesson, Draw what I learned today, and Questions to answer from the lesson. Students can write, draw, or say what they learned to their parent or guardian, but they are encouraged to draw a picture and explain to you what they have drawn.

Every so often throughout the lessons, you will see an underlined word. This word has been underlined because it will most likely need an explanation from an adult. An example from a lesson is the word prophecy. Just try your best to describe the underlined word, or you can look it up to find the definition. It is encouraged in 2nd grade for students to begin to use a dictionary to look up words.

We know that each child learns differently and at different paces. This being the case, the lessons are laid out in a day-to-day format in order to find consistency, but it is up to you as the parent/guardian to determine the actual pace and learning style of your child. You can go through the lessons faster or slower if you desire, depending on your child's level.

Opening Prayer

"Lord God prepare my heart so that it has fertile soil for the Word of God to fall on so that it will produce fruit in my life. Open my ears to hear Your Word and open my eyes to understand Your Word. In Jesus name, amen."

Scope and Sequence (Outline):

Unit 4:   The Apostles Talk About Salvation
Week 19: Acts: 4:12, Matthew 10:2, Acts 3:19, 2:38, 13:47
Week 20: Acts 16:31, Romans 5:8, 6:23, 10:9-10
Week 21: II Corinthians 5:17, 5:21, Ephesians 2:5
Week 22: I Timothy 2:1-5
Week 23: Titus 2:11-12, I Peter 2:24-25
Week 24: I John 1:9, 2:1-2

Unit 5:   Heaven and Eternity
Week 25: John 14:2, Nehemiah 9:6, 2 Kings 2:11
Week 26: Psalm 33:6, Colossians 3:1-4, Isaiah 65:17
Week 27: John 3:16, Matthew 6:19-21
Week 28: Luke 23:43, II Corinthians 5:1, Philippians 3:20-21
Week 29: Hebrews 11:16, 13:14, 2 Peter 3:13
Week 30: Revelation 21:3-4, 21

Unit 6:   Growing in Christ
Week 31: Being baptized- Matthew 28:19, Mark 1:11, 17
Week 32: Baptism in the Holy Spirit-Acts 1:8, 2:4, John. 14:16-17
Week 33: Reading the Word of God- 2 Timothy.3:16, Hebrews.4:12, Psalm.119:11
Week 34: Praying- I Thessalonians 5:16-18, 2 Chronicles. 7:14, Mark11:24
Week 35: Worshiping- Psalm 100:1-4
Week 36: Living Holy- Psalm 51:9-10, I Corinthians 6:19-20

Unit 4
Weeks 19-24

The Apostles Talk About Salvation

_____ is a child of God.

The Apostles Talk About Salvation

Opening Prayer

Weekly Memory Verse

"Nor is there salvation in any other, for there is no other name under heaven given among men by which we must be saved." Acts 4:12 (NKJV)

Copy Memory Verse

_____

_____

_____

_____

Bible Lesson

In Matthew 10:2, the Bible tells you the names of the first <u>apostles</u>. The <u>apostles</u> were the twelve disciples who followed Jesus. All of the disciples, except Judas, would go on to teach others about Jesus. The memory verse comes from the book of Acts. It tells you that Jesus is the only way to salvation. When man sinned, it broke your relationship with God. You could no longer be with God. You needed to be saved, and salvation could only come through Jesus. You can't earn salvation. You cannot be saved by another person. Salvation only comes to you through believing and accepting that Jesus, the Son of God, died and rose again.

New Words

apostles

_____

_____

_____

_____

_____

_____

Draw What You Learned

Questions

1. Who were the first apostles?

_____

_____

2. Who is the only way to salvation?

_____

_____

3. What happened when man sinned?

_____

_____

4. What happens when you believe and accept Jesus?

_____

_____

Closing Prayer

Jesus, I believe that You are the Son of God. I believe that salvation comes through You. I accept You as my Savior. Thank You Jesus! In Your mighty name, amen.

Week 19
Day 92

_____ is valued by God.

The Apostles Talk About Salvation

Opening Prayer

Weekly Memory Verse

"Nor is there salvation in any other, for there is no other name under heaven given among men by which we must be saved." Acts 4:12 (NKJV)

Read Aloud Memory Verse

Mark or color each square when completed.

1st Read Aloud

2nd Read Aloud

3rd Read Aloud

Bible Lesson

Acts 3:19 (TPT) says, "And now you must <u>repent</u> and turn back to God so that your sins will be removed, and so that times of <u>refreshing</u> will stream from the Lord's presence." When you <u>repent</u>, ask for forgiveness and turn away from your sin, God removes the sin. He doesn't remember that you even did it. When you spend time with Jesus, it helps you to be more like Him. You find that you don't want to sin anymore. The second half of the verse says that when you repent times of <u>refreshing</u> come from the Lord's presence. This <u>refreshing</u> brings you peace and strength. Jesus lifts you up and helps you to be strong when the enemy tries to tempt you to sin.

New Words

apostles

refreshing

repent

_____

_____

_____

_____

Draw What You Learned

Questions

1. According to Acts 3:19, what do you need to do?

_____

_____

2. What does <u>repent</u> mean?

_____

_____

3. What happens when you spend time with Jesus?

_____

_____

4. What does a time of <u>refreshing</u> bring you?

_____

_____

Closing Application Prayer

Lord Jesus, I repent of my sin. I'm sorry that I have sinned. I thank You for removing my sin. Help me not to sin anymore. I want to be like You, Jesus. In Your name, amen.

Week 19
Day 93

The Apostles Talk About Salvation

Opening Prayer

Weekly Memory Verse

"Nor is there salvation in any other, for there is no other name under heaven given among men by which we must be saved." Acts 4:12 (NKJV)

Copy Memory Verse

_____

_____

_____

_____

Bible Lesson

The Bible is very clear that we need to repent. In Acts 2:38 it says, "Then Peter said to them, 'Repent, and let every one of you be baptized in the name of Jesus Christ for the remission of sins; and you shall receive the gift of the Holy Spirit." It is through Jesus that our sins are forgiven. Then, the Bible says, you will receive the gift of the Holy Spirit. When Jesus left to go back to heaven, He told His disciples that it was good for them that He was leaving. He told them that because He was leaving, God was sending Holy Spirit. It was through Holy Spirit that Jesus was able to see people healed, resist temptation, and do the Father's will. When you receive the gift of Holy Spirit, you are able to do what Jesus did and more!

New Words

apostles

refreshing

repent

resist

temptation

_____

_____

Draw What You Learned

Questions

1. What happens when you <u>repent</u> and are baptized?

_____

_____

2. Why did Jesus say it was a good thing that He was leaving?

_____

_____

3. How did Jesus see people healed?

_____

_____

4. What can you do when you receive Holy Spirit?

_____

_____

Closing Prayer

Lord, I want to receive Holy Spirit. I want to do the things that Jesus did, like healing people and teaching people about the Father. In Jesus name, amen.

Week 19
Day 94

Holy Spirit Comforts_____.

The Apostles Talk About Salvation

Opening Prayer

Weekly Memory Verse

"Nor is there salvation in any other, for there is no other name under heaven given among men by which we must be saved." Acts 4:12 (NKJV)

Read Aloud Memory Verse

Mark or color each square when completed.

1st Read Aloud

2nd Read Aloud

3rd Read Aloud

Bible Lesson

The final verse this week is Acts 13:47 (TPT). It says, "This will fulfill what the Lord has commanded us: 'I have <u>destined</u> you to become a beacon light for the nations and release salvation to the ends of the earth!'" The word <u>destined</u> means to do according to a plan. God planned for you to be a light so that others could see the way to Jesus. You can be a light by loving others, praying for them, and telling them about Jesus. The verse also says that you are to send out salvation. There are people who go out to tell others about Jesus in other nations. They are called <u>missionaries</u>. When a <u>missionary</u> does this they are following this verse. They are taking salvation to the ends of the earth.

New Words

apostles

refreshing

repent

resist

temptation

destined

missionary

Draw What You Learned

Questions

1. What has God <u>destined</u> you to be?

_____

_____

2. Why does God want you to be a light?

_____

_____

3. What does <u>destined</u> mean?

_____

_____

4. What is a <u>missionary</u>?

_____

_____

Closing Application Prayer

Lord Jesus, I know that Your plan for me is to be a light to others. I know that I am supposed to tell others about You, and what You did for them. I love You! In Your name, amen.

Unit 4 Week 19: Assessment

Opening Prayer

Weekly Memory Verse

_____

_____

_____

_____

1. Who is the only way to salvation?

_____

_____

2. What does repent mean?

_____

_____

3. What happens when you spend time with Jesus?

_____

_____

4. Why did Jesus say it was a good thing that He was leaving?

_____

_____

5. What can you do when you receive Holy Spirit?

_____

_____

6. What has God destined you to be?

_____

_____

Closing Prayer

Father, I thank You for sending Jesus to be our Salvation. I can come to You because of Jesus. Help me be the light You planned for me to be. In Jesus name, amen.

GREAT JOB!

Week 20
Day 96

_____ is a child of God.

The Apostles Talk About Salvation

Opening Prayer

Weekly Memory Verse

"For the <u>wages</u> of sin is death, but the gift of God is eternal life in Christ Jesus our Lord." Romans 6:23 (NKJV)

Copy Memory Verse

_____

_____

_____

_____

Bible Lesson

The memory verse this week talks about salvation. It says that the <u>wages</u> of sin is death. Wages are a payment. When Adam and Eve sinned, they received death. It was both a physical and spiritual death. The spiritual death happened right away. They were no longer connected to God. The physical death took longer as their bodies began to die. The good news is that the verse doesn't stop there. The rest of the verse says the gift of God is eternal life in Christ Jesus. When Jesus did the will of the Father and died for you, He gave you the gift of eternal life. Even though your body will one day die, your spirit will live forever with Jesus!

New Words

wages

_____

_____

_____

_____

_____

_____

_____

Draw What You Learned

Questions

1. What are <u>wages</u>?

_____

_____

2. What is the payment of sin?

_____

_____

3. What happened to Adam and Eve when they sinned?

_____

_____

4. What is the gift of God?

_____

_____

Closing Prayer

Jesus, I am saved because of You! I was supposed to receive death because of my sin, but You took the punishment for me. I love you Jesus! In Your name, amen.

_____ is valued by God.

The Apostles Talk About Salvation

Opening Prayer

Weekly Memory Verse

"For the <u>wages</u> of sin is death, but the gift of God is eternal life in Christ Jesus our Lord." Romans 6:23 (NKJV)

Read Aloud Memory Verse

Mark or color each square when completed.

1st Read Aloud

2nd Read Aloud

3rd Read Aloud

Bible Lesson

Romans 10:9 (NKJV) says, "That if you <u>confess</u> with your mouth the Lord Jesus and believe in your heart that God has raised Him from the dead, you will be saved." It is imporant that you understand how to be saved. This verse tells you very clearly that we must <u>confess</u> Jesus. <u>Confess</u> means to say aloud. You have to let people know that you follow Jesus. That might be hard to do sometimes when people around you don't agree with you. Then, you have to believe in our heart that God raised Jesus from the dead. You must choose Jesus because you believe in Him. This is a personal decision. Nobody can believe for you. Those are the only two things you have to do to be saved. You just have to believe in and <u>confess</u> Jesus.

New Words

wages

confess

_____

_____

_____

_____

_____

Draw What You Learned

Questions

1. What does it mean to confess?

_____

_____

2. Who must you confess with your mouth?

_____

_____

3. What must you believe to be saved?

_____

_____

4. What must you do to be saved?

_____

_____

Closing Application Prayer

Lord Jesus, I confess You with mouth. I believe that You are the Son of God. I believe that You died for me and God raised You from the dead. I am Yours. In Your name, amen.

Week 20
Day 98

_____ is loved by God.

The Apostles Talk About Salvation

Opening Prayer

Weekly Memory Verse

"For the <u>wages</u> of sin is death, but the gift of God is eternal life in Christ Jesus our Lord." Romans 6:23 (NKJV)

Copy Memory Verse

_____

_____

_____

_____

Bible Lesson

    Romans 5:8 (TPT) says, "But Christ proved God's <u>passionate</u> love for us by dying in our place while we were still lost and ungodly!" <u>Passionate</u> means strong emotion. Jesus had such a strong love for you that He died in your place. It might be easy to reach out and help someone who is kind to you or loves you, but it can be hard to help someone who is mean to you or doesn't like you. Romans 5:8 tells you that Jesus died for you while you were still lost and ungodly. An ungodly person is a sinner. So, while you were still sinning and doing bad things, Jesus died for you and made a way for you to be able to change. Jesus loves you so much!

New Words

wages

confess

passionate

_____

_____

_____

_____

Draw What You Learned

Questions

1. What kind of love does Jesus have for you?

_____

_____

2. What does passionate mean?

_____

_____

3. What is an ungodly person?

_____

_____

4. What did Jesus do for us while we were lost and ungodly?

_____

_____

Closing Prayer

Jesus, You died for me while I was still a sinner. You loved me when I wasn't very lovable. Thank you for Your passionate love for me. In Your name. amen.

Holy Spirit Comforts_____.

The Apostles Talk About Salvation

Opening Prayer

Weekly Memory Verse

"For the <u>wages</u> of sin is death, but the gift of God is eternal life in Christ Jesus our Lord." Romans 6:23 (NKJV)

Read Aloud Memory Verse

Mark or color each square when completed.

1st Read Aloud

2nd Read Aloud

3rd Read Aloud

Bible Lesson

The Bible says in Acts 16:31, "So they said, 'Believe on the Lord Jesus Christ and you will be saved, you and your household.'" These words were spoken to a jailer. The Apostle Paul and Silas had been beaten and put in jail for preaching about Jesus. They were singing and praising God when all of a sudden there was an earthquake and their chains fell off and the doors of the prison opened up. The jailer was scared that all the prisoners were going to escape, but Paul and Silas told him they were all there. The jailer asked them how he could be saved. That is when Paul told him to believe on Jesus and he would be saved.

New Words

wages

confess

passionate

_____

_____

_____

_____

Draw What You Learned

Questions

1. Why were Paul and Silas beaten and put in jail?

_____

_____

2. What were Paul and Silas doing when the earth quaked?

_____

_____

3. What happened when there was an earthquake?

_____

_____

4. What did Paul tell the jailer he needed to do to be saved?

_____

_____

Closing Application Prayer

Father, I believe that Jesus is Lord. I know that He came to earth to make a way for me to come back to You. I choose to praise You like Paul and Silas. In Jesus name, amen.

Unit 4 Week 20: Assessment

Opening Prayer

Weekly Memory Verse

_____

_____

_____

_____

1. What is the payment of sin?

_____

_____

2. What is the gift of God?

_____

_____

3. Who must you confess with your mouth?

_____

_____

4. What must you believe to be saved?

_____

_____

5. What kind of love does Jesus have for you?

_____

_____

6. What did Jesus do for you while you were lost and ungodly?

_____

_____

Closing Prayer

As you finish this week, take five minutes to think about everything Jesus did for you. Tell Jesus how much You love Him. Tell Him how thankful you are for all He has done for you.

GREAT JOB!

Week 21
Day 101

_____ is a child of God.

The Apostles Talk About Salvation

Opening Prayer

Weekly Memory Verse

"Therefore, if anyone is in Christ, he is a new creation; old things have passed away; behold, all things have become new." 2 Corinthians 5:17 (NKJV)

Copy Memory Verse

_____

_____

_____

_____

Bible Lesson

The memory verse this week starts out saying, "If anyone is in Christ." You might wonder what it means to be in Christ. When you accept Jesus, when you confess Jesus with your mouth and believe that God raised Him from the dead, you are in Christ. The verse says that you become a new creation. When you are in Christ, your body doesn't change on the outside. Physically you still look the same, but your spirit changes. When Adam and Eve sinned, their spirits were <u>separated</u> from God. When Jesus died and rose again, He made a way for your spirit to be alive. When you are in Christ, your spirit is pure and <u>righteous</u>, without sin.

New Words

separated

righteous

_____

_____

_____

_____

_____

Draw What You Learned

Questions

1. How are you in Christ?

_____

_____

2. How do you become a new creation?

_____

_____

3. What happened when Adam and Eve sinned?

_____

_____

4. What does your spirit become when you are in Christ?

_____

_____

Closing Prayer

Dear Jesus, I know that I am in You because I believe that You died and rose again for me. My spirit is made new. Thank you for saving me. In Your name, amen.

Week 21
Day 102

_____ is valued by God.

The Apostles Talk About Salvation

Opening Prayer

Weekly Memory Verse

"Therefore, if anyone is in Christ, he is a new creation; old things have passed away; behold, all things have become new." 2 Corinthians 5:17 (NKJV)

Read Aloud Memory Verse

Mark or color each square when completed.

Bible Lesson

Yesterday the verse talked about how your spirit is made new when you are in Christ. The second half of the memory verse says, "Old things have passed away; behold, all things have become new." Old things are the things you used to do when you were not in Christ. This can be things like lying, stealing, talking back to your parents, and not being obedient. These are all sinful things that change when you are in Christ. When you become new, your spirit wants to do the right thing. Your flesh might not always want to do the right thing, but your spirit does. You have to <u>determine</u>, decide, that you will follow your spirit and not your flesh to do what is right.

New Words

separated

righteous

determine

_____

_____

_____

_____

Draw What You Learned

Questions

1. What passes away when you are in Christ?

_____

_____

2. What do all things become when you are in Christ?

_____

_____

3. What is an example of "old things"?

_____

_____

4. What do you have to determine?

_____

_____

Closing Application Prayer

Lord, I know that I am in Christ. I have been made new. Help me to determine that I will follow my spirit. I love you, Jesus. In Your mighty name, amen.

Week 21
Day 103

_____ is loved by God.

The Apostles Talk About Salvation

Opening Prayer

Weekly Memory Verse

"Therefore, if anyone is in Christ, he is a new creation; old things have passed away; behold, all things have become new." 2 Corinthians 5:17 (NKJV)

Copy Memory Verse

_____

_____

_____

_____

Bible Lesson

I Corinthians 5:21 continues to tell more about what Jesus did for you. It says, "For He made Him who knew no sin to be sin for us, that we might become the righteousness of God in Him." This verse says that Jesus knew no sin. Jesus never sinned. He always listened to His parents. He was always obedient. He never yelled, said no, or fought with others. He loved everyone. This verse says that Jesus became sin. He took all of your sin upon Him as if He was the one who had committed those sins, even though He didn't. When He took your sin, He made you righteous. He didn't do anything wrong, but He took your punishment as if He had.

New Words

separated

righteous

determine

_____

_____

_____

_____

Draw What You Learned

Questions

1. Who never sinned?

_____

_____

2. What does it mean that Jesus became sin?

_____

_____

3. What did you become because Jesus took your sin?

_____

_____

4. What did Jesus take that was yours even though He didn't sin?

_____

_____

Closing Prayer

Jesus, You took my punishment even though You didn't do anything wrong. When You took my sin, You made me righteous and new. Thank You Jesus! In Your name, amen.

Week 21
Day 104
Holy Spirit Comforts_____.

The Apostles Talk About Salvation

Opening Prayer

"Therefore, if anyone is in Christ, he is a new creation; old things have passed away; behold, all things have become new." 2 Corinthians 5:17 (NKJV)

Read Aloud Memory Verse

Mark or color each square when completed.

Bible Lesson

"Even when we were dead and <u>doomed</u> in our many sins, He united us into the very life of Christ and saved us by His wonderful grace!" Ephesians 2:5 (TPT) A <u>doomed</u> person is going to meet a bad end. Because you sinned you were doomed. There was no way for you to get back to God. That is why God sent Jesus! He sent Him so that you would no longer be <u>doomed</u>. When you accept Jesus and believe in Him, you are <u>united</u>, joined together, into His life. Instead of death, you have life! The Bible says that you are saved by God's grace. Grace is getting what you don't deserve. You did not deserve to have life, but Jesus gave it to you anyway.

New Words

separated

righteous

determine

doom

united

_____

_____

Draw What You Learned

Questions

1. What does it mean to be doomed?

_____

_____

2. Why were you doomed?

_____

_____

3. How are you united into Jesus?

_____

_____

4. What are you saved by?

_____

_____

Closing Application Prayer

Father, I was doomed to be without You forever because of my sin. You saved me with Your wonderful grace! Thank You for giving me what I didn't deserve. In Jesus name, amen.

Unit 4 Week 21: Assessment

Opening Prayer

Weekly Memory Verse

_____

_____

_____

_____

1. How do you become a new creation?

_____

_____

2. What does your spirit become when you are in Christ?

_____

_____

3. What passes away when you are in Christ?

_____

_____

4. Who never sinned?

_____

_____

5. What does it mean that Jesus became sin?

_____

_____

6. What are you saved by?

_____

_____

Closing Prayer

Father, I am so thankful that I am no longer doomed to a life without You. I can talk to You and know that You are always with me because of Jesus. Thank You! In Jesus name, amen.

HE LOVES ME!

Week 22 _____ is a child of God.
Day 106

The Apostles Talk About Salvation

Opening Prayer

Weekly Memory Verse

"For God is one, and there is a Mediator between God and the sons of men - the true man, Jesus, the Anointed One." 1 Timothy 2:5 (TPT)

Copy Memory Verse

_____

_____

_____

M JESUS G
A O
N D

Bible Lesson

This week's memory verse says that there is a Mediator between God and the sons of men. A mediator is someone who brings both sides together. The sons of men are all of the people that God created; that includes you. When Adam and Eve sinned, they lost the ability to have a relationship with God. Before the fall, the Bible says that Adam and Eve walked with God in the cool of the evening. They could talk to God anytime. Once sin entered the world, that relationship was stopped. Jesus, the Anointed One, is the Mediator. He made a way for both sides to come together when He died and rose again.

New Words

mediator

_____

_____

_____

_____

_____

_____

_____

Draw What You Learned

Questions

1. What is a <u>mediator</u>?

_____

_____

2. Who is the <u>mediator</u> between God and the sons of men?

_____

_____

3. Who are the sons of men?

_____

_____

4. Before the fall, when could Adam and Eve talk to God?

_____

_____

Closing Prayer

Jesus, I thank You for being the <u>mediator</u> between me and God.

You made a way for me to come back to God. I love You,

Jesus. Thank You! In Your name, amen.

_____ is valued by God.

The Apostles Talk About Salvation

Opening Prayer

Weekly Memory Verse

"For God is one, and there is a Mediator between God and the sons of men - the true man, Jesus, the Anointed One."
1 Timothy 2:5 (TPT)

Read Aloud Memory Verse

Mark or color each square when completed.

Bible Lesson

1 Timothy 2:1 (TPT) says, "Most of all, I'm writing to encourage you to pray with <u>gratitude</u> to God. Pray for all men with all forms of prayers and requests as you <u>intercede</u> with <u>intense</u> passion." Because Jesus is the mediator, you are able to talk to God, the Father, anytime you want. God loves it when you talk to Him. This verse says that we should pray with <u>gratitude</u>. <u>Gratitude</u> is a grateful attitude. Jesus has done so much for you. Every time you pray to Him, you should tell Him how thankful you are for everything He has done. Without Jesus, there would be no way for you to have a relationship with God.

New Words

mediator

gratitude

intercede

intense

_____

_____

_____

Draw What You Learned

Questions

1. How should you pray to God?

_____

_____

2. When can you pray to God?

_____

_____

3. Who makes a way for you to go to God?

_____

_____

4. What should you tell God when you pray to Him?

_____

_____

Closing Application Prayer

Father, I am so thankful for everything You have done for me. I am especially thankful for Jesus. He made a way so You and I can be together! In Jesus name, amen.

Week 22
Day 108

_____ is loved by God.

The Apostles Talk About Salvation

Opening Prayer

Weekly Memory Verse

"For God is one, and there is a Mediator between God and the sons of men - the true man, Jesus, the Anointed One."
1 Timothy 2:5 (TPT)

Copy Memory Verse

MAN   JESUS   GOD

_____

_____

_____

Bible Lesson

Yesterday you learned about the first half of 1 Timothy 2:1. It told you to pray to God with gratitude, Today's lesson talks about the rest of the verse. It says that you should pray for all men with requests and intercede with intense passion. The word intercede is to speak for someone else. The word intense is a strong feeling. So this verse is telling you that you should pray for others. It encourages you to speak to God for someone else and to do so with strong emotion. Sometimes people have very big problems and they might ask you to pray for them. You can do this because Jesus made a way. You can pray for them and God will listen!

New Words

- mediator
- gratitude
- intercede
- intense
- _____
- _____
- _____

Draw What You Learned

Questions

1. Who should you pray for?

_____

_____

2. How should you pray for all men?

_____

_____

3. What does intercede mean?

_____

_____

4. Why are you able to pray for others?

_____

_____

Closing Prayer

Jesus, because You are the mediator I can go to God, the Father and talk to Him anytime. Help me to remember to pray for others. I know You are listening. In Your name, amen.

Holy Spirit Comforts_____.

The Apostles Talk About Salvation

Opening Prayer

Weekly Memory Verse

"For God is one, and there is a Mediator between God and the sons of men - the true man, Jesus, the Anointed One."
1 Timothy 2:5 (TPT)

Read Aloud Memory Verse

Mark or color each square when completed.

Bible Lesson

1 Timothy 2:3-4 (TPT) says, "It is pleasing to our Saviour -God to pray for them. He longs for everyone to embrace His life and return to the full knowledge of the truth." God wants you to pray for others. He wants everyone to embrace His life. Embrace is to accept. God wants everyone to accept the life Jesus is offering them. It is a life that is full of truth. The truth is that God loves everyone and does not want anyone to spend eternity away from Him. God wants you to pray that people will accept Jesus and live for Him. This means that they repent of their sin and make Jesus their Lord.

New Words

mediator

gratitude

intercede

intense

embrace

_____

_____

Draw What You Learned

Questions

1. What does God want you to do for others?

_____

_____

2. What does embrace mean?

_____

_____

3. What does God want you and others to embrace?

_____

_____

4. What is the truth?

_____

_____

Closing Application Prayer

Father God, I choose to embrace Your life and believe in the truth that Jesus died for me and rose again. I choose to pray for others so they will know the truth. In Jesus name, amen.

Unit 4 Week 22: Assessment

Opening Prayer

Weekly Memory Verse

_____

_____

_____

_____

1. What is a mediator?

_____

_____

2. Who is the mediator between God and the sons of men?

_____

_____

3. How should you pray to God?

_____

_____

4. What does intercede mean?

_____

_____

5. Why are you able to pray for others?

_____

_____

6. What does God want you and others to embrace?

_____

_____

Closing Prayer

Jesus, I am so thankful for all You did for me. I choose to follow the plan You have for my life. I choose to tell others about You and to pray for them. In Your mighty name, amen.

GREAT JOB!

Week 23
Day 111

_____ is loved by God.

The Apostles Talk About Salvation

Opening Prayer

Weekly Memory Verse

"God's marvelous grace has <u>manifested</u> in person, bringing salvation for everyone." Titus 2:11 (TPT)

Copy Memory Verse

_____

_____

_____

_____

Bible Lesson

The memory verse this week talks about God's wonderful grace. Grace is getting what you don't deserve. It's kind of like getting a prize that you didn't earn. The verse says His grace was <u>manifested</u> in person. The word <u>manifest</u> means to be seen. God's marvelous grace could be seen in a person. That person is Jesus, the Son of God. When Jesus came to earth, He took your punishment and you got blessings instead. You didn't deserve those blessings, but you received them anyway. That is God's grace. The rest of the verse says that God's grace, through Jesus, brought salvation to everyone.

New Words

manifest

_____

_____

_____

_____

_____

_____

Draw What You Learned

Questions

1. What is grace?

_____

_____

2. What does <u>manifest</u> mean?

_____

_____

3. Who was grace <u>manifested</u> in?

_____

_____

4. What did you receive when Jesus took your punishment?

_____

_____

Closing Prayer

Father, thank You for Your grace being <u>manifested</u> in Jesus. Thank You for Your grace. Thank You for giving me blessings instead of the punishment I deserve. In Jesus name, amen.

_____ is valued by God.

The Apostles Talk About Salvation

Opening Prayer

Weekly Memory Verse

"God's marvelous grace has <u>manifested</u> in person, bringing salvation for everyone." Titus 2:11(TPT)

Read Aloud Memory Verse

Mark or color each square when completed.

Bible Lesson

Titus 2:12 (TPT) says, "This same grace teaches us how to live each day as we turn our backs on ungodliness and <u>indulgent</u> lifestyles, and it <u>equips</u> us to live self-controlled, upright, godly lives in this present age." God's grace does so much for you. It helps you to turn your back on sin. If you have an <u>indulgent</u> lifestyle, you allow yourself to do whatever you want. God's grace teaches you that every day you need to look to Jesus for what He wants you to do. This verse also says that God's grace will <u>equip</u> you and, give you the ability to live a godly life. When you have a godly life, you show self-control. You live your life according to the Bible.

New Words

manifest

indulgent

equips

_____

_____

_____

_____

Draw What You Learned

[ ]

Questions

1. What does God's grace teach you?

_____

_____

2. What should you turn your back on?

_____

_____

3. What does an <u>indulgent</u> lifestyle look like?

_____

_____

4. What does <u>equip</u> mean?

_____

_____

Closing Application Prayer

Father, thank You for Your grace. Thank You for teaching me to turn my back on sin. I choose to live a godly life and show self-control. In Jesus name, amen.

Jesus loves_____.

The Apostles Talk About Salvation

Opening Prayer

Weekly Memory Verse

"God's marvelous grace has <u>manifested</u> in person, bringing salvation for everyone." Titus 2:11(TPT)

God's
Marvelous
Grace

Copy Memory Verse

_____

_____

_____

_____

Bible Lesson

Our lesson today comes from 1 Peter 2:24 (TPT). It says, "He Himself carried our sins in His body on the cross so that we would be dead to sin and live for righteousness. Our instant healing flowed from His <u>wounding</u>." Jesus took your sin upon Himself. He did this so you would no longer sin. Jesus wants you to make good choices. He does not want you to sin. He knows that sin brings death and pain. Jesus does not want that for you. Jesus wants you to live in righteousness. He wants you to be a light to others and tell them about Jesus. The last part of the verse talks about Jesus' <u>wounding</u>, being hurt. We can have healing in our body because Jesus was <u>wounded</u> for us.

New Words

manifest

indulgent

equips

wounding

_____

_____

_____

Draw What You Learned

Questions

1. Who carried your sins in His body?

_____

_____

2. Why did Jesus take your sin upon Himself?

_____

_____

3. What does sin bring?

_____

_____

4. What is <u>wounding</u>?

_____

_____

Closing Prayer

Jesus, thank You for taking my sin upon Yourself on the cross so that I can live forever. I don't have to sin anymore. Help me to live righteously. I love you Jesus. In Your mighty name, amen.

Holy Spirit Comforts_____.

The Apostles Talk About Salvation

Opening Prayer

Weekly Memory Verse

"God's marvelous grace has <u>manifested</u> in person, bringing salvation for everyone." Titus 2:11 (TPT)

Read Aloud Memory Verse

Mark or color each square when completed.

Bible Lesson

This week finishes with 1 Peter 2:25. It says, "You were like sheep that continually <u>wandered</u> away, but now you have returned to the true Shepherd of your lives - the kind <u>Guardian</u> who lovingly watches over your souls." This verse says that you are like a sheep. Sheep wander, walk away and get lost, a lot. Sheep need a shepherd to watch over them and keep them safe. Without Jesus, it is very easy for the enemy to tempt you to sin and walk away from God. Jesus came to be the Shepherd that you need. The Bible says that Jesus is the <u>Guardian</u>, protector, of your soul. He lovingly watches over you and takes care of you.

New Words

manifest

indulgent

equips

wounding

wandered

Guardian

_____

Draw What You Learned

Questions

1. Who is like a sheep?

_____

_____

2. Who is the Shepherd?

_____

_____

3. Why do sheep need a Shepherd?

_____

_____

4. What is a guardian?

_____

_____

Closing Application Prayer

Jesus, thank You for coming to be my Shepherd. You protect me and keep me safe. Help me to stay close to You. Thank You for being my protector. In Your name, amen.

Unit 4 Week 23: Assessment

Opening Prayer

Weekly Memory Verse

_____

_____

_____

_____

1. What is grace?

_____

_____

2. What did you receive when Jesus took your punishment?

_____

_____

3. What does God's grace teach you?

_____

_____

4. Why did Jesus take your sin upon Himself?

_____

_____

5. Who is the Shepherd?

_____

_____

6. Why do sheep need a shepherd?

_____

_____

Closing Prayer

Jesus, Thank You for Your grace. Your grace gave me blessings instead of punishment. I want to tell others about Your grace. Show me how to help others. In Your name, amen.

YOU DID GREAT!

_____ is a child of God.

The Apostles Talk About Salvation

Opening Prayer

Weekly Memory Verse

"If we <u>confess</u> our sins, He is faithful and just to forgive us our sins and to <u>cleanse</u> us from all unrighteousness."

1 John 1:9 (NKJV)

Copy Memory Verse

_____

_____

_____

_____

Bible Lesson

The memory verse this week tells you exactly what happens when you <u>confess</u> your sins to God. <u>Confess</u> means to tell. You might wonder why you need to <u>confess</u> your sins to God. You should <u>confess</u> your sins because the Bible tells you to. This verse tells you that when you <u>confess</u>, Jesus is faithful and <u>just</u> to forgive you. Jesus is always faithful. He will always do what He says. If the Bible says that Jesus will forgive you, than you can be sure He will. The word <u>just</u> means righteous or true. Jesus is both faithful and righteous. He will forgive you when you <u>confess</u> your sins to Him.

New Words

confess

cleanse

just

_____

_____

_____

_____

Draw What You Learned

Questions

1. What does it mean to <u>confess</u>?

_____

_____

2. Who should you <u>confess</u> your sins to?

_____

_____

3. What does <u>just</u> mean?

_____

_____

4. What is Jesus faithful and <u>just</u> to do?

_____

_____

Closing Prayer

Jesus, You are always faithful. Whatever Your Word says that You will do, I know that it will be done. I <u>confess</u> my sins to You. Thank You for forgiving me. In Your precious name, amen.

_____ is valued by God.

The Apostles Talk About Salvation

Opening Prayer

Weekly Memory Verse

"If we <u>confess</u> our sins, He is faithful and just to forgive us our sins and to <u>cleanse</u> us from all unrighteousness."

1 John 1:9 (NKJV)

Read Aloud Memory Verse

Mark or color each square when completed.

Bible Lesson

Today's lesson will continue to look at the memory verse. When Jesus forgives your sins, He also <u>cleanses</u> you from all unrighteousness. <u>Cleanse</u> means to make clean. Unrighteousness is sin and that sin can be things like being disobedient, stealing, lying, or other things that go against the Word of God. When you <u>confess</u> your sins to Jesus, He promises to forgive you; He cleans all of the sins away and makes you new. To Jesus, it is as if you never sinned. Jesus died on the cross, so that you could have that freedom to be forgiven.

New Words

confess

cleanse

just

_____

_____

_____

_____

Draw What You Learned

Questions

1. What happens when Jesus forgives your sins?

_____

_____

2. What does <u>cleanse</u> mean?

_____

_____

3. What is unrighteousness?

_____

_____

4. Who will never remember your sins?

_____

_____

Closing Application Prayer

Jesus, You are always faithful. I know that when I <u>confess</u> my sins to You, I have Your forgiveness. You make me clean. Thank You for making me new. In Your mighty name, amen.

_____ is loved by God.

The Apostles Talk About Salvation

Opening Prayer

Weekly Memory Verse

"If we <u>confess</u> our sins, He is faithful and just to forgive us our sins and to <u>cleanse</u> us from all unrighteousness."

1 John 1:9 (NKJV)

Copy Memory Verse

_____

_____

_____

_____

Bible Lesson

1 John 2:1 (NKJV) says, "My little children, these things I write to you, so that you may not sin. And if anyone sins, we have an <u>Advocate</u> with the Father, Jesus Christ the righteous." Spending time with God and reading the Bible will help you not to sin. If you do sin, you can be sure that you will be forgiven. This verse says that if you sin, you have an <u>Advocate</u>. His name is Jesus. An <u>advocate</u> is someone who supports you. As an <u>Advocate</u>, Jesus goes to the Father for you. He reminds the Father that forgiveness is yours because He died for you. You are made righteous because of Jesus.

New Words

confess

cleanse

advocate

_____

_____

_____

_____

Draw What You Learned

Questions

1. What will help you not to sin?

_____

_____

2. What is an <u>advocate</u>?

_____

_____

3. Who is our <u>Advocate</u>?

_____

_____

4. How does Jesus <u>advocate</u> for you?

_____

_____

Closing Prayer

Father, You loved me so much that before I ever needed to be forgiven, You had already made a way. I am so thankful that You forgive me! In Jesus name, amen.

Holy Spirit Comforts_____.

The Apostles Talk About Salvation

Opening Prayer

Weekly Memory Verse

"If we <u>confess</u> our sins, He is faithful and just to forgive us our sins and to <u>cleanse</u> us from all unrighteousness."

1 John 1:9 (NKJV)

Read Aloud Memory Verse

Mark or color each square when completed.

Bible Lesson

Yesterday you read 1 John 2:1. Today the lesson will be on the next verse. 1 John 2:2 (TPT) says, "He is the <u>atoning</u> sacrifice for our sins, and not only for ours but also for the sins of the whole world." God had a plan from the beginning of the world. He knew that man would sin. He knew that man would need a Savior. So, before He ever created man, Jesus was the sacrifice man would need. The word <u>atoning</u> means to make a wrong right. An <u>atoning</u> <u>sacrifice was needed because man sinned, or did wrong.</u> Jesus wasn't just the sacrifice for you. He was the sacrifice for everyone in the whole world!

New Words

- confess
- cleanse
- advocate
- atoning
- _____
- _____
- _____

Draw What You Learned

Questions

1. Who is the atoning sacrifice for your sins?

_____

_____

2. When did God make the plan to send a Savior for man?

_____

_____

3. What does the word atoning mean?

_____

_____

4. Who was Jesus the sacrifice for?

_____

_____

Closing Application Prayer

Father, You loved me so much that before I ever needed to be forgiven, You had already made a way. I am so thankful that You forgive me! In Jesus name, amen.

Unit 4 Week 24: Assessment

Opening Prayer

Weekly Memory Verse

_____

_____

_____

_____

1. Who should you confess your sins to?

_____

_____

2. What is Jesus faithful and just to do?

_____

_____

3. What happens when Jesus forgives your sins?

_____

_____

4. How does Jesus advocate for you?

_____

_____

5. When did God make the plan to send a Savior for man?

_____

_____

6. Who was Jesus the sacrifice for?

_____

_____

Closing Prayer

Jesus, I have learned so much about salvation. I know that You made a way for me and everyone in the world. I am so thankful for Your sacrifice. I love You, Jesus! In Your name, amen.

HE LOVES ME!

Unit 5
Weeks 25-30

Heaven and Eternity

Week 25
Day 121

_____ is a child of God.

Heaven and Eternity

Opening Prayer

"In My Father's house are many <u>mansions</u>; if it were not so, I would have told you. I go to <u>prepare</u> a place for you."
John 14:2 (NKJV)

Copy Memory Verse

_____

_____

_____

_____

Bible Lesson

In this unit, you will learn about both heaven and earth. The memory verse this week comes from John 14:2. Jesus spoke these words. He was getting ready to leave His disciples and go back to Heaven. He called Heaven His Father's house. Heaven is filled with the Father. It is a place that is full of the glory of the Lord. It is where the children of God go when their physical bodies die. Jesus told His disciples that in Heaven there are many <u>mansions</u>. A <u>mansion</u> is a gigantic, or very large house. It is true, because Jesus always speaks the truth.

New Words

mansions

prepare

_____

_____

_____

_____

_____

Draw What You Learned

Questions

1. What was Jesus about to do when He spoke John 14:2?

_____

_____

2. According to John 14:2, what is heaven?

_____

_____

3. What is there a lot of in Heaven?

_____

_____

4. Who always speaks the truth?

_____

_____

Closing Prayer

Father, I thank You for making Heaven. I know that one day I will go there to be with You. Thank You Jesus for making a way so I can go to Heaven. In Your name, amen.

_____ is valued by God.

Heaven and Eternity

Opening Prayer

Weekly Memory Verse

"In My Father's house are many <u>mansions</u>; if it were not so, I would have told you. I go to <u>prepare</u> a place for you."
John 14:2 (NKJV)

Read Aloud Memory Verse

Mark or color each square when completed.

1st Read Aloud

2nd Read Aloud

3rd Read Aloud

Bible Lesson

Yesterday the lesson talked about the Father's house, Heaven. Today the rest of the verse will be discussed. Jesus told the disciples that there were many <u>mansions</u> in Heaven. You might wonder who those <u>mansions</u> are for. Jesus told the disciples that He was going back to the Father's house to <u>prepare</u>, or make, a place for them. He was going to <u>prepare mansions</u> for the disciples. Jesus died for everyone, not just the disciples. So, if Jesus is <u>preparing</u> a <u>mansion</u> for the disciples, than that means He is making a <u>mansion</u> for you too!

New Words

mansions

prepare

_____

_____

_____

_____

_____

Draw What You Learned

Questions

1. What does the word prepare mean?

_____

_____

2. Who was Jesus preparing a mansion for?

_____

_____

3. Where was Jesus going to prepare a place?

_____

_____

4. Were the disciples the only ones who would have a mansion?

_____

_____

Closing Application Prayer

Jesus, I know You have gone to Heaven to prepare a place for me. I thank You for my mansion in Heaven. Help me to tell others about You! In Your name, amen.

Week 25
Day 123

_____ is loved by God.

Heaven and Eternity

Opening Prayer

Weekly Memory Verse

"In My Father's house are many <u>mansions</u>; if it were not so, I would have told you. I go to <u>prepare</u> a place for you."
John 14:2 (NKJV)

Copy Memory Verse

_____

_____

_____

_____

Bible Lesson

"You alone are the Lord; You have made heaven, The heaven of heavens, with all their host, The earth and everything on it, The seas and all that is in them, And You <u>preserve</u> them all. The host of heaven worships You." Nehemiah 9:6 (NKJV) This verse clearly shows that God has created everything. He made the earth, the skies, and the heavens. God made everything on the earth, like people, animals, and plants. He made everything in the sea; God, the Father, made all the hosts - the sun, moon, and stars. They worship God and we should worship God too! The verse says that God <u>preserves</u> them all. <u>Preserve</u> is to protect or keep in good condition. God protects all that He created.

New Words

mansions

prepare

preserve

_____

_____

_____

_____

Draw What You Learned

Questions

1. What did God create?

_____

_____

2. What in the earth did God create?

_____

_____

3. What are the hosts?

_____

_____

4. What does God <u>preserve</u>?

_____

_____

Closing Prayer

Father, thank You for creating me. You created everything. You protect and watch over me, Your creation. I love You, Jesus! In Your name, amen.

Holy Spirit Comforts_____.

Heaven and Eternity

Opening Prayer

Weekly Memory Verse

"In My Father's house are many <u>mansions</u>; if it were not so, I would have told you. I go to <u>prepare</u> a place for you."
John 14:2 (NKJV)

Read Aloud Memory Verse

Mark or color each square when completed.

1st
Read
Aloud

2nd
Read
Aloud

3rd
Read
Aloud

Bible Lesson

2 Kings 2:11 tells us about Heaven as a place. It says, "Then it happened, as they continued on and talked, that suddenly a <u>chariot</u> of fire appeared with horses of fire, and separated the two of them; and Elijah went up by a <u>whirlwind</u> into heaven." Elijah was a prophet. He had been told by God that he would be taken to Heaven. This verse shows that Heaven is a place people go to. It is important to know that only those who accept Jesus as their Savior will go to Heaven. Elisha was a follower of the prophet Elijah. He was with Elijah when this happened. While they were walking a <u>chariot</u> (a cart driven by a horse) that was on fire picked up Elijah and separated him from Elisha. Then in a <u>whirlwind</u>, a small tornado, Elijah was taken to Heaven.

New Words

mansions

prepare

preserve

chariot

whirlwind

_____

_____

Draw What You Learned

Questions

1. Who was Elijah?

_____

_____

2. Who was Elisha?

_____

_____

3. What was Elijah taken in?

_____

_____

4. Where was Elijah taken?

_____

_____

Closing Application Prayer

Father, Thank You for showing me that Heaven is a place. I know that one day I will go to Heaven to be with You forever because I have Jesus as my Savior. In Jesus name, amen.

Unit 5 Week 25: Assessment

Opening Prayer

Weekly Memory Verse

_____

_____

_____

_____

1. According to John 14:2, what is Heaven?

_____

_____

2. Who always speaks the truth?

_____

_____

3. Where was Jesus going to prepare a place?

_____

_____

4. What did God create?

_____

_____

5. What does God preserve?

_____

_____

6. Where was Elijah taken?

_____

_____

Closing Prayer

Father, You created the earth and heaven. Heaven is a place where I will one day spend eternity with You. Help me to complete my plan on earth. In Jesus name, amen.

GREAT JOB!

_____ is a child of God.

Heaven and Eternity

Opening Prayer

Weekly Memory Verse

"Christ's <u>resurrection</u> is your <u>resurrection</u> too. This is why we are to <u>yearn</u> for all that is above, for that's where Christ sits <u>enthroned</u> at the place of all power, honor, and authority!" Colossians 3:1 (TPT)

Copy Memory Verse

_____

_____

_____

_____

Bible Lesson

<u>Resurrection</u> is to come back from the dead. The memory verse this week states that when Christ came back from the dead, so did you! Because Jesus rose again, you will too. Your spirit will live with Jesus in Heaven for eternity The word <u>yearn</u> means to really want something. The verses say that you should really want the things that are above. Those are the things that are in Heaven. You should be desiring to do the work of the Lord. Things like spending time talking to God, praising and worshiping God, helping a friend, and going to church are ways for you to <u>yearn</u> for things that are above.

New Words

resurrection

yearn

enthroned

_____

_____

_____

_____

Draw What You Learned

Questions

1. What does <u>resurrection</u> mean?

_____

_____

2. Where will your spirit live for eternity?

_____

_____

3. What does <u>yearn</u> mean?

_____

_____

4. What should you <u>yearn</u> for?

_____

_____

Closing Prayer

Jesus, thank You that because You rose from the dead, I will too! When I die, my spirit will live with You in Heaven for eternity. I love You, Jesus. In Your name, amen.

_____ is valued by God.

Heaven and Eternity

Opening Prayer

Weekly Memory Verse

"Christ's <u>resurrection</u> is your <u>resurrection</u> too. This is why we are to <u>yearn</u> for all that is above, for that's where Christ sits <u>enthroned</u> at the place of all power, honor, and authority!" Colossians 3:1 (TPT)

Read Aloud Memory Verse

Mark or color each square when completed.

Bible Lesson

The second half of the memory verses focuses on where Christ is. When Jesus rose again, He was on the earth for a little while. Then, He <u>ascended</u>, went up, into Heaven. The verse tells you that Jesus is there, in Heaven. He sits <u>enthroned</u>. When someone is <u>enthroned</u>, they are put on a throne. Jesus is sitting on a real throne in Heaven. He has a place of power. Jesus is all powerful. When He died and rose again, He took all power away from satan. Jesus has all the honor. He deserves your praise and respect. Jesus has all authority. He has the right to make demands and those demands have to be obeyed.

New Words

resurrection

yearn

enthroned

ascended

_____

_____

_____

Draw What You Learned

Questions

1. Where was Jesus when He first rose again?

_____

_____

2. Where did Jesus ascend to?

_____

_____

3. What does it mean to be enthroned?

_____

_____

4. What three things does Jesus have?

_____

_____

Closing Application Prayer

Jesus, You ascended to Heaven and are seated on a throne.

You have all power, honor, and authority. Thank You for saving

me. In Your mighty name, amen.

Week 26
Day 128

_____ is loved by God.

Heaven and Eternity

Opening Prayer

Weekly Memory Verse

"Christ's <u>resurrection</u> is your <u>resurrection</u> too. This is why we are to <u>yearn</u> for all that is above, for that's where Christ sits <u>enthroned</u> at the place of all power, honor, and authority!" Colossians 3:1 (TPT)

Copy Memory Verse

_____

_____

_____

_____

Bible Lesson

Isaiah 65:17 (NKJV) says, "For behold, I create new Heavens and a new earth; And the <u>former</u> shall not be remembered or come to mind." God is saying in this verse that He is going to create a new Heaven and a new earth. This world can be hard to live in sometimes. There is so much pain and destruction that happened when Adam and Eve sinned. God never planned for the world to be like this. One day He is going to create a new Heaven and a new earth. Then, there the <u>former</u> things, the things in the past, will not be remembered. Things like trouble, pain, and destruction will be forgotten.

New Words

resurrection

yearn

enthroned

ascended

former

_____

_____

Draw What You Learned

Questions

1. What new things is God going to create?

_____

_____

2. Why would we need a new world?

_____

_____

3. When did pain and destruction enter the earth?

_____

_____

4. What does former mean?

_____

_____

Closing Prayer

Father, You are always good. You did not create this world to be a place where people have pain. I thank You that one day You will make a new Heaven and earth! In Jesus name, amen.

Holy Spirit comforts_____.

Heaven and Eternity

Opening Prayer

Weekly Memory Verse

"Christ's <u>resurrection</u> is your <u>resurrection</u> too. This is why we are to <u>yearn</u> for all that is above, for that's where Christ sits <u>enthroned</u> at the place of all power, honor, and authority!" Colossians 3:1 (TPT)

Read Aloud Memory Verse

Mark or color each square when completed.

Bible Lesson

Psalms 33:6 (NKJV) says, "By the word of the Lord the heavens were made, And all the hosts of them by the breath of His mouth." Heaven is where the angels live. It is where you will spend eternity with God. Heaven was created through God's spoken word. He spoke and it came to be. God, the Father is so powerful that His breath was all it took to create Heaven. We have the same power to create with our words. That is why it is so important that we speak the same way Jesus did. We should speak everything with love and according to what God wants.

New Words

resurrection

yearn

enthroned

ascended

former

_____

_____

Draw What You Learned

Questions

1. How was Heaven made?

_____

_____

2. Who lives in Heaven?

_____

_____

3. What do our words have?

_____

_____

4. How should we speak our words?

_____

_____

Closing Application Prayer

Lord, I thank You for the power You displayed when You created the earth. Help me to remember that my words have power and I should speak the way you want me to. In Jesus name, amen.

Unit 5 Week 26: Assessment

Opening Prayer

Weekly Memory Verse

_____

_____

_____

_____

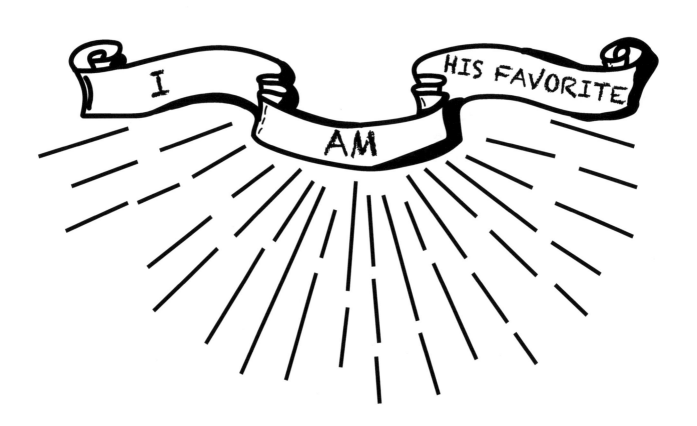

1. Where will your spirit live for eternity?

_____

_____

2. What should you yearn for?

_____

_____

3. Where did Jesus ascend to?

_____

_____

4. What new things is God going to create?

_____

_____

5. When did pain and destruction enter the earth?

_____

_____

6. What do our words have?

_____

_____

Closing Prayer

Father, I am learning all about Your power. You are so powerful that You created Heaven with just Your words. I choose to follow You and Your ways. In Jesus name, amen.

YOU DID GREAT!

Week 27
Day 131

_____ is a child of God.

Heaven and Eternity

Opening Prayer

Weekly Memory Verse

"For God so loved the world that He gave His only <u>begotten</u> Son, that whoever believes in Him should not <u>perish</u> but have everlasting life." John 3:16 (NKJV)

Copy Memory Verse

_____

_____

_____

_____

Bible Lesson

God loves you! No one loves you as much as God loves You! He loves you so much that He gave His only <u>begotten</u> Son for you. <u>Begotten</u> means to bring to life. God is Jesus' Father. Imagine how much love God has for you that He was willing to give up His Son for you! This verse tells you that while God loves you, He also loves the entire world. Every person in the world is loved by God. Your parents, your brothers and sisters, your family, and your friends are loved by God. He Sent His Son to die for the whole world. It's God's desire that every person in the world would believe in Jesus as the Son of God and repent.

New Words

begotten

perish

_____

_____

_____

_____

_____

Draw What You Learned

Questions

1. How do you know that God loves you?

_____

_____

2. Who does God love?

_____

_____

3. What does begotten mean?

_____

_____

4. What did God do for the whole world?

_____

_____

Closing Prayer

Lord, I am learning how much You love me. You love me so much that You sent Your Son to die for me! Help me to tell others about Your love. In Jesus name, amen.

Week 27
Day 132

_____ is valued by God.

Heaven and Eternity

Opening Prayer

Weekly Memory Verse

"For God so loved the world that He gave His only <u>begotten</u> Son, that whoever believes in Him should not <u>perish</u> but have everlasting life." John 3:16 (NKJV)

Read Aloud Memory Verse

Mark or color each square when completed.

Bible Lesson

The memory verse tells you that God loved you so much, He sent His Son to die for you. He did this because He wanted to spend eternity with you in Heaven. The word <u>perish</u> means to die. This is not talking about your physical body. It is talking about your spirit. God did not want your spirit to die and be separated from Him forever. When you receive Jesus as your Savior, Heaven becomes your eternal home. You may live on this earth for awhile, but not forever. One day, your physical body will die and you will spend forever with Jesus in Heaven. The Father made this way for you because He loves you so much!

New Words

begotten

perish

_____

_____

_____

_____

_____

Draw What You Learned

Questions

1. Whom did God love so much that He sent Jesus?

_____

_____

2. Why did God send Jesus?

_____

_____

3. What becomes your eternal home when you receive Jesus?

_____

_____

4. What does the word perish mean?

_____

_____

Closing Application Prayer

Father, thank You for sending Your Son, Jesus, to die for me. I know that when my physical body dies, my spirit will live forever with You in Heaven. I love you! In Jesus name, amen.

Week 27
Day 133

_____ is loved by God.

Heaven and Eternity

Opening Prayer

Weekly Memory Verse

"For God so loved the world that He gave His only <u>begotten</u> Son, that whoever believes in Him should not <u>perish</u> but have everlasting life." John 3:16 (NKJV)

Copy Memory Verse

_____

_____

_____

Bible Lesson

Matthew 6:19 says, "Do not lay up for yourselves <u>treasures</u> in earth, where moth and rust destroy and where thieves break in and steal;" When you think of <u>treasures</u>, you might think of buried gold, or shiny valuable stones. The <u>treasures</u> you store up on this earth cannot go to Heaven with you. Here, on earth, anything can happen to your <u>treasure</u>. Moths might destroy it or thieves could break in and steal it. You should not spend all your time trying to get things here on this earth. You should not keep everything you have for youself. You might think you are keeping it safe, and then it could disappear. The things of this world will not last, but the things in Heaven will last forever.

New Words

begotten

perish

treasure

_____

_____

_____

_____

Draw What You Learned

Questions

1. Where should you not store your <u>treasure</u>?

_____

_____

2. What can destroy your <u>treasure</u> if you store it on earth?

_____

_____

3. Who could steal your <u>treasure</u>?

_____

_____

4. How long will things in Heaven last?

_____

_____

Closing Prayer

Father, I know that treasures on this earth will not last forever. I cannot take anything from earth with me when I go to Heaven. I choose to do things for you instead of me. In Jesus name, amen.

Week 27
Day 134

Holy Spirit comforts_____.

Heaven and Eternity

Opening Prayer

Weekly Memory Verse

"For God so loved the world that He gave His only <u>begotten</u> Son, that whoever believes in Him should not <u>perish</u> but have everlasting life." John 3:16 (NKJV)

Read Aloud Memory Verse

Mark or color each square when completed.

Bible Lesson

Matthew 6:20 (NKJV) says, "but lay up for yourselves <u>treasures</u> in Heaven, where neither moth nor rust destroys and where thieves do not break in and steal." The Bible says to store your <u>treasure</u> in Heaven, where it will last for eternity. Nothing can destroy <u>treasure</u> that is in Heaven. <u>Treasure</u> in Heaven comes from doing things for the Lord on earth. It can come in all different ways. Helping a friend in need will earn <u>treasure</u> in Heaven. Giving to the work of the Lord, spending time with Jesus in worship, sharing a favorite toy with someone who doesn't have anything to play with, or praying for a person who is sick are all ways to build <u>treasure</u> in Heaven.

New Words

begotten

perish

treasure

_____

_____

_____

_____

Draw What You Learned

Questions

1. Where should you store your treasure?

_____

_____

2. Why should you store your treasure in Heaven?

_____

_____

3. What is one way to store up treasure in Heaven?

_____

_____

4. What can giving to the work of the Lord do for you?

_____

_____

Closing Application Prayer

Jesus, I want to store up my treasure in Heaven. I know that when I do things for You, I am storing up treasure where it can't be destroyed or stolen. In Your name, amen.

Unit 5 Week 27: Assessment

Opening Prayer

Weekly Memory Verse

_____

_____

_____

_____

1. How do you know that God loves you?

_____

_____

2. What becomes your eternal home when you receive Jesus?

_____

_____

3. Why did God send Jesus?

_____

_____

4. Why should you store your treasure in Heaven?

_____

_____

5. How long will things in Heaven last?

_____

_____

6. What is one way to store up treasure in Heaven?

_____

_____

Closing Prayer

Jesus, You came to earth so that I could go to Heaven. I want to spend eternity with You. I choose to follow You and store up my treasure in Heaven. In Your name, amen.

HE LOVES ME!

Week 28
Day 136

_____ is a child of God.

Heaven and Eternity

Opening Prayer

Weekly Memory Verse

"And Jesus said to him, 'Assuredly, I say to you, today you will be with Me in Paradise.'" Luke 23:43 (NKJV)

Copy Memory Verse

_____

_____

_____

_____

Bible Lesson

The memory verse tells you about when Jesus was crucified. Jesus was on the cross between two thieves. One thief thought only of himself. He mocked or made fun of Jesus. He said that if Jesus was God, He should be able to save Himself. He wanted to know why Jesus didn't take Himself off the cross and save the two thieves too. The other thief was different. He believed that Jesus was the Son of God. He asked Jesus to remember him when Jesus entered into His Kingdom. That Kingdom was Paradise, or Heaven. Jesus used the word assuredly. That means definitely. Jesus told the thief that he would definitely be able to be with Jesus in Paradise.

New Words

Paradise

assuredly

_____

_____

_____

_____

_____

Draw What You Learned

Questions

1. What did the thief that mocked Jesus want Jesus to do?

_____

_____

2. What did the thief that believed in Jesus ask?

_____

_____

3. What is Paradise?

_____

_____

4. What did Jesus tell the thief who believed?

_____

_____

Closing Prayer

Jesus, thank You for going to the cross for me. You could have taken Yourself off the cross, but You stayed on for me. I love You, Jesus. In Your name, amen.

Week 28
Day 137

_____ is valued by God.

Heaven and Eternity

Opening Prayer

Weekly Memory Verse

"And Jesus said to him, '<u>Assuredly</u>, I say to you, today you will be with Me in <u>Paradise</u>.'" Luke 23:43 (NKJV)

Read Aloud Memory Verse

Mark or color each square when completed.

1st Read Aloud   2nd Read Aloud   3rd Read Aloud

Bible Lesson

Yesterday you learned about the two thieves on the cross and how one of them asked Jesus to let him enter into Jesus' Kingdom. Jesus told the thief that he would be with Jesus in <u>Paradise</u>. Jesus says the same thing to you. You cannot get to Heaven by just living a good life. The thief did not live a good life. He was being put to death because he had done bad things. That didn't matter to Jesus. What mattered to Jesus was that the thief believed that Jesus was the Son of God. The Bible is clear that you will go to Heaven if you believe that Jesus is the Son of God and you repent of your sins. If you do those two things, you will be with Jesus in <u>Paradise</u> when you die.

New Words

Paradise

assuredly

_____

_____

_____

_____

Draw What You Learned

Questions

1. What does Jesus say to you?

_____

_____

2. Does living a good life get you to Heaven?

_____

_____

3. Why was the thief being put to death?

_____

_____

4. Why did Jesus tell the thief he would be with Jesus in Paradise?

_____

_____

Closing Application Prayer

Jesus, I know that just living a good life will not get me to Heaven.

The only way that I can go to Heaven is to repent and believe that

You are the Son of God. Thank You, Jesus, for making a way!

Week 28
Day 138

_____ is loved by God.

Heaven and Eternity

Opening Prayer

Weekly Memory Verse

"And Jesus said to him, 'Assuredly, I say to you, today you will be with Me in Paradise.'" Luke 23:43 (NKJV)

Copy Memory Verse

_____

_____

_____

_____

Bible Lesson

   2 Corinthians 5:1 (NKJV) says, "For we know that if our earthly house, this tent, is destroyed, we have a building from God, a house not made with hands, eternal in the Heavens." Your human body will not last forever. The verse says that your body is your earthly house that is like a tent. It won't be used anymore. You, however, have a God-built home. That home is Heaven. Man did not make Heaven, God did. God made Heaven for you to be able to live with Him for eternity or forever. No one will be able to destroy Heaven. The things that man makes will not last forever, but the things God makes will be for eternity. He loves you with an everlasting love, and He cannot wait to be with you in eternity.

New Words

Paradise

assuredly

_____

_____

_____

_____

_____

Draw What You Learned

Questions

1. What is your body compared to in 2 Corinthians 5:1?

_____

_____

2. Who built Heaven?

_____

_____

3. How long will Heaven last?

_____

_____

4. Who can destroy Heaven?

_____

_____

Closing Prayer

Father, thank You for making a place where my spirit can live with You forever! I want to spend all my time on earth living for You! In Jesus name, amen.

Holy Spirit comforts_____.

Heaven and Eternity

Opening Prayer

Weekly Memory Verse

"And Jesus said to him, 'Assuredly, I say to you, today you will be with Me in Paradise.'" Luke 23:43 (NKJV)

Read Aloud Memory Verse

Mark or color each square when completed.

Bible Lesson

Philippians 3:20 (TPT) says, "But we are a colony of heaven on earth as we cling tightly to our Life-Giver, the Lord Jesus Christ," A colony is a group of people who live in one place but have their citizenship (real home) in another place. You live on this earth, but your citizenship is in Heaven. You live and grow up on earth, but your real home is Heaven. The verse goes on to say that you cling tightly to your Life-Giver. Jesus is your Life-Giver. Without Jesus, you would not be a citizen of Heaven. You would have no chance to be with God after you die. You would spend eternity without God. His will is for all to come to Him and be with Him in Heaven.

New Words

Paradise

assuredly

colony

citizenship

_____

_____

_____

Draw What You Learned

Questions

1. What is a colony?

_____

_____

2. What is citizenship?

_____

_____

3. What are we a colony of?

_____

_____

4. Who gives us life?

_____

_____

Closing Application Prayer

Jesus, You are my Life-Giver. I cling to You. Without You I would have an eternity of being far away from You. I choose You, Jesus. Thank You for saving me. In Your name, amen.

Unit 5 Week 28: Assessment

Opening Prayer

Weekly Memory Verse

_____

_____

_____

_____

1. What did Jesus tell the thief who believed?

_____

_____

2. Does just living a good life get you to Heaven?

_____

_____

3. Why did Jesus tell the thief he would be with Jesus in Paradise?

_____

_____

4. Who made Heaven?

_____

_____

5. How long will Heaven last?

_____

_____

6. Who gives us life?

_____

_____

Closing Prayer

Jesus, because of Your sacrifice, Heaven will one day be my eternal home. I believe in You! I believe that You are the Son of God. I will spend eternity with You. In Your name, amen.

GREAT JOB!

Week 29
Day 141

_____ is a child of God.

Heaven and Eternity

Opening Prayer

Weekly Memory Verse

"But now they desire a better, that is, a heavenly country. Therefore God is not <u>ashamed</u> to be called their God, for He has prepared a city for them." Hebrews 11:16 (NKJV)

Copy Memory Verse

_____

_____

_____

_____

Bible Lesson

In this unit, you have been reading <u>passages</u>, verses, about Heaven and eternity. The memory verse this week tells that God has prepared a city for His children. This verse is talking about the heroes of the faith, people like Enoch, Noah, Abraham and Sarah. They all were honored because they believed that God would do the impossible in their lives. They all walked closely with God. Walking closely with God means that you spend time with Him. You care more about what God thinks than what others think. These men and women wanted to be a part of Heaven and what God was doing instead of the evil of the world. You can be a hero of the faith too! You just need to listen to and follow Holy Spirit.

New Words

passages

ashamed

_____

_____

_____

_____

_____

Draw What You Learned

Questions

1. Who has God prepared a city for?

_____

_____

2. Who was one of heroes of the faith?

_____

_____

3. What did the heroes of the faith believe?

_____

_____

4. What does it mean to walk closely with God?

_____

_____

Closing Prayer

Father, I know that You have a plan for my life. You want me to walk closely with You. I choose to spend time with You every day. In Jesus name, amen.

_____ is valued by God.

Heaven and Eternity

Opening Prayer

Weekly Memory Verse

"But now they desire a better, that is, a heavenly country. Therefore God is not <u>ashamed</u> to be called their God, for He has prepared a city for them." Hebrews 11:16 (NKJV)

Read Aloud Memory Verse

Mark or color each square when completed.

Bible Lesson

Yesterday you read about the heroes of the faith and the city that God has prepared for them. The verse also says that God is not <u>ashamed</u> of them. If you are ashamed of people, you are embarrassed by them. You don't want to be around them. God was not embarrassed to be the God of these heroes of the faith and He is not <u>ashamed</u> to be your God either. He loves you so much! He is happy when He sees your desire to be with Him. His desire is to always be with you. The verses says God prepared a city. That city is called Heaven. He prepared it for all of His children who follow Him. God wants to spend eternity in Heaven with you and all the people that love Him.

New Words

passages

ashamed

_____

_____

_____

_____

_____

Draw What You Learned

Questions

1. What does the word <u>ashamed</u> mean?

_____

_____

2. Why is God not <u>ashamed</u> to be your God?

_____

_____

3. What is the name of the city God prepared?

_____

_____

4. Who does God want to spend eternity with?

_____

_____

Closing Application Prayer

Father, thank You for not being <u>ashamed</u> to be my God. Thank You for preparing a city for me to spend eternity with You. I love You! In Jesus name, amen.

Week 29
Day 143

Heaven and Eternity

Opening Prayer

Weekly Memory Verse

"But now they desire a better, that is, a heavenly country. Therefore God is not <u>ashamed</u> to be called their God, for He has prepared a city for them." Hebrews 11:16 (NKJV)

Copy Memory Verse

_____

_____

_____

_____

Bible Lesson

Hebrews 13:14 (TPT) says, "For we have no city here on earth to be our <u>permanent</u> home, but we seek the city that is destined to come." The word <u>permanent</u> means forever. If something is <u>permanent</u> it is not going to change. Here on earth there is no <u>permanent</u> home for God's children. You are here for a short time. One hundred years is so tiny compared to eternity. Eternity is forever. God created a permanent home for all of His children. It is a city that will last forever. That <u>permanent</u> home is called Heaven. God, the Father, lives in Heaven. When you go to Heaven, you will live with Him for eternity.

New Words

passages

ashamed

permanent

_____

_____

_____

_____

Draw What You Learned

Questions

1. What does the word <u>permanent</u> mean?

_____

_____

2. What cannot be found on earth?

_____

_____

3. How long is eternity?

_____

_____

4. What is your <u>permanent</u> home called?

_____

_____

Closing Prayer

Father, You created a <u>permanent</u> city called Heaven for me. I know that one day I will live there with You forever. Thank You for making a way for me. In Jesus name, amen.

Week 29
Day 144

Holy Spirit comforts_____.

Heaven and Eternity

Opening Prayer

Weekly Memory Verse

"But now they desire a better, that is, a heavenly country. Therefore God is not <u>ashamed</u> to be called their God, for He has prepared a city for them." Hebrews 11:16 (NKJV)

Read Aloud Memory Verse

Mark or color each square when completed.

Bible Lesson

2 Peter 3:13 (NKJV) says, "Nevertheless we, according to His promise, look for new heavens and a new earth in which righteousness dwells." The Bible says that God made a promise. God always does what He promises. God promised that there would be a new Heaven and a new earth. This new place will not have pain, problems, or evil. The verse uses the words "look for." These words mean to expect. The Bible is clear that we can expect that this new Heaven and earth will be created. It says that righteousness will <u>dwell</u> there. The word <u>dwell</u> means to live or stay. Righteousness will always be in the new Heaven and earth.

New Words

- passages
- ashamed
- permanent
- dwell
- _____
- _____
- _____

Draw What You Learned

Questions

1. What promise did God make?

_____

_____

2. What does God always do with His promises?

_____

_____

3. What does look for mean?

_____

_____

4. What will always dwell in the new Heaven and earth?

_____

_____

Closing Application Prayer

Father, thank You for Your Word. Your Word is full of promises. I know that all of Your promises will come to pass because You always tell the truth. You are faithful. In Jesus name, amen.

Unit 5 Week 29: Assessment

Opening Prayer

Weekly Memory Verse

_____

_____

_____

_____

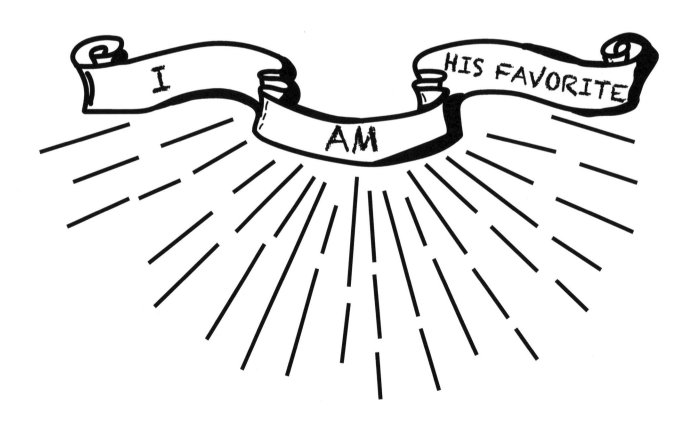

1. Who has God prepared a city for?

_____

_____

2. What does it mean to walk closely with God?

_____

_____

3. What is the name of the city God prepared?

_____

_____

4. How long is eternity?

_____

_____

5. What promise did God make?

_____

_____

6. What will always dwell in the new Heaven and earth?

_____

_____

Closing Prayer

Father, the Bible tells me that You have created a home for me that will last forever. That home is called Heaven. I will live there with You forever. In Jesus name, amen.

YOU DID GREAT!

_____ is a child of God.

Heaven and Eternity

Opening Prayer

Weekly Memory Verse

"The twelve gates are twelve pearls - each gate made of one pearl. And the street of the city was pure gold, clear as <u>crystal</u>." Revelation 21:21 (TPT)

Copy Memory Verse

_____

_____

_____

_____

Bible Lesson

In the final week of this unit, you will read some <u>descriptions</u> of Heaven. A <u>description</u> tells what things look like. The memory verse starts out by describing the gates of Heaven. There are twelve gates. In the past, a lot of cities had gates. Do you remember that there were twelve tribes of Israel, and Jesus chose twelve disciples. Twelve gates is a lot of gates for a city. In Heaven, the gates are beautiful. They are made of pearl. A pearl is a shiny white gem that is made in the shell of a mollusk. The Bible says that the pearls are so large each gate is made from only one pearl. That is a huge pearl! God has prepared such a beautiful place for you in Heaven. He loves you so much. You are so valuable to Him.

New Words

crystal

descriptions

_____

_____

_____

_____

_____

Draw What You Learned

Questions

1. What is a <u>description</u>?

_____

_____

2. How many gates are in Heaven?

_____

_____

3. What is a pearl made from?

_____

_____

4. What is each gate made of?

_____

_____

Closing Prayer

Father, I know that one day I will see those beautiful pearl gates.

The gates will be amazing, but the real joy will be being in

Heaven with You. I love you! In Jesus name, amen.

_____ is valued by God.

Heaven and Eternity

Opening Prayer

Weekly Memory Verse

"The twelve gates are twelve pearls - each gate made of one pearl. And the street of the city was pure gold, clear as crystal." Revelation 21:21 (TPT)

Read Aloud Memory Verse

Mark or color each square when completed.

1st Read Aloud

2nd Read Aloud

3rd Read Aloud

Bible Lesson

Yesterday you read about the gates of Heaven. They are made of a single pearl. The rest of the verse says that the streets of Heaven are made of pure gold. Gold is a very beautiful and valuable resource on earth. In Heaven, people are the beautiful and valuable resources. God, the Father, used gems and gold to build His city. The verse says that the gold is so pure that it looks as clear as crystal. Crystal is a type of glass that you can look through. The gold in Heaven is just like crystal. It is so clear that you can see right through it. Everything in Heaven is pure and beautiful. He has prepared a beautiful place for you.

New Words

crystal

descriptions

_____

_____

_____

_____

_____

Draw What You Learned

Questions

1. What are the streets of Heaven made of?

_____

_____

2. What is the valuable resource in Heaven?

_____

_____

3. What is <u>crystal</u>?

_____

_____

4. What does the gold in Heaven look like?

_____

_____

Closing Application Prayer

Father, thank You for not being ashamed to be my God. Thank You for preparing a city for me to spend eternity with You. I love You! In Jesus name, amen.

Week 30
Day 148

_____ is loved by God.

Heaven and Eternity

Opening Prayer

Weekly Memory Verse

"The twelve gates are twelve pearls - each gate made of one pearl. And the street of the city was pure gold, clear as crystal." Revelation 21:21 (TPT)

Copy Memory Verse

_____

_____

_____

_____

Bible Lesson

Revelation 21:3 (TPT) says, "And I heard a loud voice from the Heaven, saying: 'Behold, the tabernacle of God is with men, and He will dwell with them, and they shall be His people. God Himself will be with them and be their God.'" The tabernacle was the dwelling place for God in the Old Testament. God was kept separate because He is holy and man sinned. Only the high priest could go in to God's dwelling place. People did not have access to God. When Jesus came, He made a way for you to be with God all the time. You can pray and talk to God whenever you want. In Heaven, God is not separate from you. When you go to live there you live in the same place as God. He is your God and you are His child.

New Words

- passages
- ashamed
- tabernacle
- _____
- _____
- _____
- _____

Draw What You Learned

Questions

1. What is a <u>tabernacle</u>?

_____

_____

2. What could only the high priest do?

_____

_____

3. Why was God separated from man?

_____

_____

4. Who made a way for you to be with God?

_____

_____

Closing Prayer

Father, I'm so glad that I am not separated anymore. I'm so thankful that Jesus made a way for You and me to be together. In Heaven I will live with You. In Jesus name, amen.

Week 30
Day 149

Holy Spirit comforts_____.

Heaven and Eternity

Opening Prayer

"The twelve gates are twelve pearls - each gate made of one pearl. And the street of the city was pure gold, clear as crystal." Revelation 21:21 (TPT)

Read Aloud Memory Verse

Mark or color each square when completed.

1st Read Aloud

2nd Read Aloud

3rd Read Aloud

Bible Lesson

Revelation 21:4 (NKJV) continues from yesterday. It says, "And God will wipe away every tear from their eyes; there shall be no more death, nor sorrow, nor crying. There shall be no more pain, for the former things have passed away." This is a description of how people will be in Heaven. The Bible says that in Heaven there will be no more tears. On earth, you see a lot of sad things. There may even be times when you cry. In Heaven, there will be no more crying. People will not die. God will take away all sorrow. Sorrow is suffering. When you go to Heaven, there will be no suffering. There will be love, peace, and joy in the presence of your God. All the things of this earth will be gone, replaced with God's glory.

New Words

passages

ashamed

tabernacle

sorrow

_____

_____

_____

Draw What You Learned

Questions

1. What will there be no more of in Heaven?

_____

_____

2. What does sorrow mean?

_____

_____

3. Will there be suffering and death in Heaven?

_____

_____

4. What will be replaced with God's glory?

_____

_____

Closing Application Prayer

Lord, I am so excited to know that there is no pain, death, and crying in Heaven. I will never know sadness again. Thank You Jesus for making a way for me to go to Heaven. In Your name, amen.

Unit 5 Week 30: Assessment

Opening Prayer

Weekly Memory Verse

_____

_____

_____

_____

1. How many gates are in Heaven?

_____

_____

2. What is each gate made of?

_____

_____

3. What are the streets of Heaven made of?

_____

_____

4. What is the most valuable resource in Heaven?

_____

_____

5. Why was man separated from God?

_____

_____

6. What will there be no more of in Heaven?

_____

_____

Closing Prayer

Father, Heaven is a beautiful place! I am so excited to one day live there forever. I know that while I am on earth, You have a plan for me. Help me to do Your plan. In Your name, amen.

HE LOVES ME!

Unit 6
Weeks 31-36

Growing in Christ

_____ is loved by God.

Growing in Christ

Opening Prayer

Weekly Memory Verse

"Go therefore and make <u>disciples</u> of all nations, baptizing them in the name of the Father and of the Son and of the Holy Spirit," Matthew 28:19 (NKJV)

Copy Memory Verse

_____

_____

_____

_____

Bible Lesson

In this unit you will learn about growing in Christ. In the memory verse, you read that Jesus told His <u>disciples</u> to go and make <u>disciples</u> of all nations. A <u>disciple</u> is a follower of someone or something. The <u>disciples</u> were not going out to get people to follow them, they were making disciples of Jesus. Everywhere they went, they told people about Jesus and how Jesus was the Son of God Who died for their sins. The <u>disciples</u> taught the people and then the people taught others. You can be a follower of Jesus too! You can learn about Jesus at church, from reading the Bible, and spending time talking with Jesus.

New Words

disciples

_____

_____

_____

_____

_____

_____

Draw What You Learned

Questions

1. What is a disciple?

_____

_____

2. Where did Jesus tell His disciples to go and make disciples?

_____

_____

3. Who did the disciples teach others to follow?

_____

_____

4. How can you learn about Jesus?

_____

_____

Closing Prayer

Jesus, You made a way for me to be Your disciple. I can learn from You by praying, reading the Bible, and going to church. I want to know You more. In Your name, amen.

Week 31
Day 152

_____ is valued by God.

Growing in Christ

Opening Prayer

"Go therefore and make <u>disciples</u> of all nations, baptizing them in the name of the Father and of the Son and of the Holy Spirit," Matthew 28:19 (NKJV)

Read Aloud Memory Verse

Mark or color each square when completed.

1st Read Aloud

2nd Read Aloud

3rd Read Aloud

Bible Lesson

Yesterday you read about making <u>disciples</u>. Today's lesson is about being baptized. Jesus told His <u>disciples</u> to make <u>disciples</u> and then baptize them. Jesus was baptized before He went into full-time ministry. When you are baptized, you are following Jesus' example. The <u>disciples</u> taught others how to be saved and then, like John the Baptist, they would baptize people. They baptized them in the name of the Father, the Son, and the Holy Spirit. All three parts of God - Father, Son, and Holy Spirit, play a part as you walk out your Christian life. God, the Father, sent His Son to die for you. Jesus, the Son, died and rose again for you. Holy Spirit lives in you to help you as you live your Christian life.

New Words

disciples

_____

_____

_____

_____

_____

_____

Draw What You Learned

Questions

1. What should you do after you accept Jesus as Savior?

_____

_____

2. Whose example do we follow when we are baptized?

_____

_____

3. In Whose name are you baptized?

_____

_____

4. What does Holy Spirit do for you?

_____

_____

Closing Application Prayer

Father, thank You for sending Jesus to save me. I know that because I am saved, Holy Spirit is here to help me live my life as a Christian. I choose to listen to Holy Spirit. In Jesus name, amen.

Week 31
Day 153

Growing in Christ

Opening Prayer

Weekly Memory Verse

"Go therefore and make <u>disciples</u> of all nations, baptizing them in the name of the Father and of the Son and of the Holy Spirit," Matthew 28:19 (NKJV)

Copy Memory Verse

_____

_____

_____

_____

Bible Lesson

Mark 1:11(NKJV) says, "Then a voice came from heaven, 'You are My <u>beloved</u> Son, in whom I am well pleased.'" This verse comes right after Jesus was baptized by John the Baptist. God, the Father, spoke from Heaven. He was so proud of Jesus. The Father loves Jesus so much. He called Jesus His <u>beloved</u> Son. <u>Beloved</u> means deeply loved. You are God's <u>beloved</u> child too! He loves you so much! John the Baptist wanted Jesus to baptize Him. He knew that Jesus was the <u>Messiah</u>, Savior of the world. Jesus, however, knew that to be obedient He would need to be baptized by John. Jesus did everything the Father told Him to do. You should follow Jesus' example and listen to God.

New Words

- disciples
- beloved
- Messiah
- _____
- _____
- _____
- _____

Draw What You Learned

Questions

1. Who spoke from heaven?

_____

_____

2. What did the Father call Jesus?

_____

_____

3. Who baptized Jesus?

_____

_____

4. Who did Jesus follow and listen to?

_____

_____

Closing Prayer

Jesus, You gave me a great example of how to be obedient.
You were always obedient to the Father. Help me to be
obedient too! In Your mighty name, amen.

Week 31
Day 154

Holy Spirit comforts_____.

Growing in Christ

Opening Prayer

"Go therefore and make <u>disciples</u> of all nations, baptizing them in the name of the Father and of the Son and of the Holy Spirit," Matthew 28:19 (NKJV)

Read Aloud Memory Verse

Mark or color each square when completed.

1st Read Aloud

2nd Read Aloud

3rd Read Aloud

Bible Lesson

Jesus was tested for forty days after He was baptized. He then began to preach and tell people to repent. In Mark 11:17 (NKJV) it says, "Then Jesus said to them, 'Follow Me and I will make you become fishers of men.'" Jesus said this to two brothers who were fishermen. They knew how to catch fish. Jesus told them that He was going to teach them how to catch men. This does not mean that they were going to throw nets around men and force them to do what they say. Being a fisher of men meant teaching others how to be saved. The disciples would spend a little over three years with Jesus learning how to help others know Jesus.

New Words

- disciples
- beloved
- Messiah
- _____
- _____
- _____
- _____

Draw What You Learned

Questions

1. How long was Jesus tested after He was baptized?

_____

_____

2. What did Jesus say to the two fishermen?

_____

_____

3. What does it mean to be a fisher of men?

_____

_____

4. How long would the disciples spend with Jesus?

_____

_____

Closing Application Prayer

Jesus, You died so I could be free. Help me to be a fisher of men. Help me to tell those I love about You and what You did for them. In Your name, amen.

Unit 6 Week 31: Assessment

Opening Prayer

Weekly Memory Verse

_____

_____

_____

_____

1. What is a disciple?

_____

_____

2. Who did the disciples teach others to follow?

_____

_____

3. What should you do after you accept Jesus as Savior?

_____

_____

4. In Whose name are you baptized?

_____

_____

5. What did the Father call Jesus?

_____

_____

6. What does it mean to be a fisher of men?

_____

_____

Closing Prayer

Father, this week I learned that being baptized is one way to grow in Jesus. I learned that I can be a fisher of men. I choose to listen to You and follow You. In Jesus name, amen.

GREAT JOB!

Week 32
Day 156

_____ is loved by God.

Growing in Christ

Opening Prayer

Weekly Memory Verse

"But you shall receive power when the Holy Spirit has come upon you; and you shall be witnesses to Me in Jerusalem, and in all Judea and Samaria, and to the end of the earth."   Acts 1:8 (NKJV)

Copy Memory Verse

_____

_____

_____

_____

Bible Lesson

This week you will learn about the Holy Spirit. The memory verse says that the Holy Spirit would come upon you. Jesus told the disciples that God was sending a helper. He said that it was good that He went back to Heaven because then the helper would come. When you are filled with Holy Spirit, you are filled with power. It was through Holy Spirit that Jesus did His miracles. When Jesus came to earth He was God but He was also man. He did not do miracles, give prophetic words, and <u>discern</u> (know and understand) people's thoughts on His own. He did all of that through the power of Holy Spirit. You can be filled with Holy Spirit and see great miracles too!

New Words

discern

_____

_____

_____

_____

_____

_____

Draw What You Learned

Questions

1. Who did the Father send as a helper?

_____

_____

2. What are you filled with when you are filled with Holy Spirit?

_____

_____

3. How did Jesus perform miracles while on the earth?

_____

_____

4. What does discern mean?

_____

_____

Closing Prayer

Father, thank You for sending Holy Spirit to be a helper. I want to be filled with Holy Spirit. I want to see people receive miracles because of Holy Spirit. In Jesus name, amen.

_____ is valued by God.

Growing in Christ

Opening Prayer

Weekly Memory Verse

"But you shall receive power when the Holy Spirit has come upon you; and you shall be witnesses to Me in Jerusalem, and in all Judea and Samaria, and to the end of the earth."   Acts 1:8 (NKJV)

Read Aloud Memory Verse

Mark or color each square when completed.

1st
Read
Aloud

2nd
Read
Aloud

3rd
Read
Aloud

Bible Lesson

Yesterday you learned that when the Holy Spirit comes, He brings power. He gave Jesus power to heal and do miracles. The second half of the verse talks about what God wants you to do with that power. Jesus told the disciples that they would be His witnesses in every part of the world. When Holy Spirit comes, He helps you complete the plan that God has for you. The disciples were to take the good news of what Jesus did, along with healings and miracles, and share them all over the world so that others would know and receive Jesus as their Savior. Just like the disciples, you can share the good news and see Holy Spirit work through you with healings and miracles.

New Words

discern

_____

_____

_____

_____

_____

_____

Draw What You Learned

Questions

1. Where did Jesus tell His disciples they would be a witness?

_____

_____

2. What does Holy Spirit help you do?

_____

_____

3. What were the disciples supposed to share?

_____

_____

4. Why were the disciples to share the good news?

_____

_____

Closing Application Prayer

Father, You have an awesome plan for me. I need Holy Spirit to help me complete my plan. Thank You for sending Holy Spirit to me. In Jesus, name, amen.

_____ is loved by God.

Growing in Christ

Opening Prayer

Weekly Memory Verse

"But you shall receive power when the Holy Spirit has come upon you; and you shall be witnesses to Me in Jerusalem, and in all Judea and Samaria, and to the end of the earth."   Acts 1:8 (NKJV)

Copy Memory Verse

_____

_____

_____

_____

Bible Lesson

Acts 2:4 (NKJV) says, " And they were all filled with the Holy Spirit and began to speak with other tongues, as the Spirit gave them <u>utterance</u>." The Holy Spirit was poured out upon those who waited for Him. Every person who was waiting was filled. When they were filled with Holy Spirit some things happened. First, they began to speak in other tongues. When Holy Spirit moves upon you, you will speak in a Heavenly language. The Bible says that your Heavenly language is to edify your spirit. An <u>utterance</u> is a spoken word or statement. Holy Spirit gave them the words to say. When you speak in the Holy Spirit you are speaking to the Lord in your Heavenly language.

New Words

discern

utterance

_____

_____

_____

_____

_____

Draw What You Learned

Questions

1. Who was the Holy Spirit poured out upon?

_____

_____

2. What happened first when Holy Spirit came?

_____

_____

3. What does the word utterance mean?

_____

_____

4. What is speaking in tongues?

_____

_____

Closing Prayer

Father, thank You for sending Holy Spirit. I know that You sent Him to be a helper. I want to be filled with Holy Spirit and speak in tongues. In Jesus name, amen.

Week 32
Day 159

Holy Spirit comforts_____.

Growing in Christ

Opening Prayer

"But you shall receive power when the Holy Spirit has come upon you; and you shall be witnesses to Me in Jerusalem, and in all Judea and Samaria, and to the end of the earth."   Acts 1:8 (NKJV)

Read Aloud Memory Verse

Mark or color each square when completed.

1st Read Aloud

2nd Read Aloud

3rd Read Aloud

Bible Lesson

John 14:16-17 (NKJV) says, "And I will pray the Father, and He will give you another Helper, that He may <u>abide</u> with you forever - the Spirit of truth, whom the world cannot receive because it neither sees Him nor knows Him; but you know Him, for He dwells with you and will be in you." Jesus spoke these words. He told His disciples that He would pray and the Father would send a Helper. That Helper is Holy Spirit. The Bible says that Holy Spirit will <u>abide</u>, or live, with you forever. You can receive Him because you know Him. You know Him because you believe that Jesus is the Son of God and He is your Savior. The Bible says the world cannot receive Holy Spirit because they can't see or know Him.

New Words

discern

utterance

abide

_____

_____

_____

_____

Draw What You Learned

[drawing box]

Questions

1. According to John 14:16-17, who will <u>abide</u> with you forever?

_____

_____

2. Who sent Holy Spirit?

_____

_____

3. What does the word <u>abide</u> mean?

_____

_____

4. Why can the world not receive Holy Spirit?

_____

_____

Closing Application Prayer

Father God, thank You for sending Holy Spirit. I know that I can receive Him because I know Him. He lives with me and will always be with me. In Jesus name, amen.

Unit 6 Week 32: Assessment

Opening Prayer

Weekly Memory Verse

_____

_____

_____

_____

1. Who did the Father send as a helper?

_____

_____

2. What are you filled with when you are filled with Holy Spirit?

_____

_____

3. Where did Jesus tell His disciples they would be a witness?

_____

_____

4. Who was the Holy Spirit poured out upon?

_____

_____

5. What is speaking in tongues?

_____

_____

6. According to John 14:16-17, who will abide with you forever?

_____

_____

Closing Prayer

Jesus, it is because of You that the Holy Spirit was poured out. When You left and went back to Heaven, You sent Holy Spirit to help. Thank You, Holy Spirit, for living with me always. In Jesus name, amen.

YOU DID GREAT!

_____ is loved by God.

Growing in Christ

Opening Prayer

Weekly Memory Verse

"All scripture is given by <u>inspiration</u> of God, and is <u>profitable</u> for <u>doctrine</u>, for <u>reproof</u>, for correction, for instruction in righteousness," 2 Timothy 3:16 (NKJV)

Copy Memory Verse

_____

_____

_____

_____

Bible Lesson

The Bible is God's Word. It is given by <u>inspiration</u>. When something is <u>inspired</u> by someone, it comes from them. The Bible was <u>inspired</u> by God. All of the Bible came from God. The Old Testament tells of creation and how man sinned and was separated from God. It prophecies about the future and the Messiah who will come. The New Testament tells about the Messiah coming, the prophecies He fulfilled, and how you can grow in Christ. The Bible was written by men, but those men were led by the Holy Spirit. When you read the Bible, you should pray and ask Holy Spirit to show you what He wants you to learn from the scriptures. This is one way you can grow in Christ.

New Words

inspiration

profitable

doctrine

reproof

_____

_____

_____

Draw What You Learned

Questions

1. What is God's Word called?

_____

_____

2. Who inspired the Bible?

_____

_____

3. Who were the writers of the Bible led by?

_____

_____

4. What does reading the Bible help you to do?

_____

_____

Closing Prayer

Father, thank You for giving me the Word of God. I know that it was inspired by You. All of the words in the Bible came from You. Help me to read Your Word every day. In Jesus name, amen.

_____ is valued by God.

Growing in Christ

Opening Prayer

Weekly Memory Verse

"All scripture is given by <u>inspiration</u> of God, and is <u>profitable</u> for <u>doctrine</u>, for <u>reproof</u>, for correction, for instruction in righteousness," 2 Timothy 3:16 (NKJV)

Read Aloud Memory Verse

Mark or color each square when completed.

Bible Lesson

The memory verse continues by telling you what the Word of God is for. It says that the Word is <u>profitable</u> for <u>doctrine</u>. <u>Profitable</u> means good for and <u>doctrine</u> is teaching. The Word of God is good for teaching you. It is also good for <u>reproofing</u> and correcting. <u>Reproofing</u> is showing what is wrong and correcting, or helping to make the wrong things right. When you read the Word of God, Holy Spirit shows you the things that need to change in your life. Finally, reading the Bible gives you instructions on how to live a life of righteousness. God wants you to be a light to others. When you follow His Word, you will show others the right way to live and be an example of Jesus.

New Words

- inspiration
- profitable
- doctrine
- reproof
- _____
- _____
- _____

Draw What You Learned

Questions

1. Who does the Word of God teach?

_____

_____

2. What is <u>reproofing</u>?

_____

_____

3. What does Holy Spirit show you when you read the Bible?

_____

_____

4. What instructions does the Bible give you?

_____

_____

Closing Application Prayer

Heavenly Father, I thank You for giving me the Bible. I know that it comes from You. Help me to read Your Word every day and live a righteous life. In Jesus name, amen.

Week 33
Day 163

_____ is loved by God.

Growing in Christ

Opening Prayer

"All scripture is given by <u>inspiration</u> of God, and is <u>profitable</u> for <u>doctrine</u>, for <u>reproof</u>, for correction, for instruction in righteousness," 2 Timothy 3:16 (NKJV)

Copy Memory Verse

_____

_____

_____

_____

Bible Lesson

Hebrews 4:12 (NKJV) says, "For the Word of God is living and powerful, and sharper than any two-edged sword, <u>piercing</u> even to the division of soul and spirit, and of joints and marrow, and is a discerner of the thoughts and <u>intents</u> of the heart." God's Word is alive. It is powerful. When you read the Bible, it shows you things that are in your heart. It shows the intent of your heart. Intent is the purpose or reason for doing something. Sometimes you might do something nice, but the reason is not right. You might share a toy with your sibling because you have to, when you should be doing it out of love. The Bible shows you what you need to change so that you can be more like Jesus.

New Words

inspiration

profitable

doctrine

reproof

_____

_____

_____

Draw What You Learned

Questions

1. What does pierce mean?

_____

_____

2. What is one word to describe the Word of God?

_____

_____

3. What does intent mean?

_____

_____

4. What helps you to change and be like Jesus?

_____

_____

Closing Prayer

Heavenly Father, thank You for Your Word. When I read it, it shows me things in my heart that need to change. Help me to read Your Word everyday. In Jesus name, amen.

Week 33
Day 164

Holy Spirit comforts_____.

Growing in Christ

Opening Prayer

Read Aloud Memory Verse

Mark or color each square when completed.

Bible Lesson

Psalm 119:11(NKJV) says, "Your Word I have hidden in my heart, That I might not sin against You." Hiding God's Word in your heart is so important for you. You hide God's Word in your heart by reading, <u>meditating</u> (thinking on it), and memorizing it. Before you start reading the Bible, pray and ask the Lord to speak to your heart and reveal the scriptures to you. It is not enough to just read the Bible. You need to take time to think about it. Ask Holy Spirit what you need to learn from the scripture that you are reading. Let the Lord show you how you need to change. Then, spend time memorizing the Bible. With each weekly verse, take time to really memorize the verse and practice it any time that you can. When you hide God's Word in your heart, you stay out of trouble and spend more time doing good for the Lord.

New Words

profitable

doctrine

reproof

penetrate

motives

reveal

meditating

Draw What You Learned

Questions

1. Where should you hide God's Word?

_____

_____

2. What are three ways to hide God's Word in your heart?

_____

_____

3. Who should you ask to teach you as you read the Bible?

_____

_____

4. What happens when you hide God's Word in your heart?

_____

_____

Closing Application Prayer

Jesus, help me to hide Your Word in my heart. I choose to read the Bible every day. Help me to learn from what I read. Help me to memorize Your Word. In Your name, amen.

Unit 6 Week 33: Assessment

Opening Prayer

Weekly Memory Verse

_____

_____

_____

_____

1. What is God's Word called?

_____

_____

2. Who inspired the Bible?

_____

_____

3. What instructions does the Bible give you?

_____

_____

4. What is one word to describe the Word of God?

_____

_____

5. What are three ways to hide God's Word in your heart?

_____

_____

6. What happens when you hide God's Word in your heart?

_____

_____

Closing Prayer

Heavenly Father, this week I have learned why I need to read Your Word every day. Help me to understand as I read Your Word, and let it change me to be like You! In Jesus name, amen.

HE LOVES ME!

_____ is loved by God.

Growing in Christ

Opening Prayer

Weekly Memory Verse

"Rejoice always, 17 pray without <u>ceasing</u>, 18 in everything give thanks; for this is the will of God in Christ Jesus for you."
1 Thessalonians 5:16-18 (NKJV)

Copy Memory Verse

_____

_____

_____

_____

Bible Lesson

One way to grow in Christ is to pray. The memory verse this week talks about praying without <u>ceasing</u>. <u>Ceasing</u> means to stop. You should pray without stopping. That does not mean that you have to sit in your room all day and pray. There are many time throughout your day when you can talk to God. Spending time with the Father in prayer is the best way to start your day. This way He can tell you how to complete the plan He has for you that day. Thanking God for the meals you have before you eat is another great way to pray throughout the day. When you find you need patience with a sibling or friends, or before you take a test you can talk with God. The more time you spend with God in prayer, the more you become like Him!

New Words

ceasing

_____

_____

_____

_____

_____

_____

Draw What You Learned

Questions

1. What does <u>ceasing</u> mean?

_____

_____

2. How should you pray?

_____

_____

3. What is one way you can talk to God throughout the day?

_____

_____

4. What happens when you spend time in prayer with God?

_____

_____

Closing Prayer

Heavenly Father, You have said that I should pray without <u>ceasing</u>. I know that You are always listening. Help me to take everything to You in prayer. In Jesus name, amen.

_____ is valued by God.

Growing in Christ

Opening Prayer

Weekly Memory Verse

"Rejoice always, 17 pray without <u>ceasing</u>, 18 in everything give thanks; for this is the will of God in Christ Jesus for you."

1 Thessalonians 5:16-18 (NKJV)

Read Aloud Memory Verse

Mark or color each square when completed.

 1st Read Aloud

 2nd Read Aloud

 3rd Read Aloud

Bible Lesson

Yesterday you read about praying without <u>ceasing</u>. The rest of the verse gives you two important things to remember. First, you should "rejoice always". That goes together with the second which is, "in everything give thanks." There is always something that you can be thankful for. Even when sad things happen, you can be thankful that God is with you and never leaves you. The Bible says that it is God's will for you to rejoice, be thankful and pray without <u>ceasing</u>. When you do these three things, you are able to live for the Lord in a way that shows others Jesus. People need to know that Jesus loves them and wants to save them. When you follow these verses, you will help others to know Jesus.

New Words

ceasing

_____

_____

_____

_____

_____

_____

_____

Draw What You Learned

Questions

1. What should you always do?

_____

_____

2. Who is always with you, even in sad times?

_____

_____

3. What three things are God's will for you to do?

_____

_____

4. What is one thing you can give thanks to God for right now?

_____

_____

Closing Application Prayer

Jesus, because You died for me and rose again, I can have a relationship with the Father. I choose to rejoice, give thanks, and pray without <u>ceasing</u>. In Your name, amen.

Week 34
Day 168

_____ is loved by God.

Growing in Christ

Opening Prayer

Weekly Memory Verse

"Rejoice always, 17 pray without <u>ceasing</u>, 18 in everything give thanks; for this is the will of God in Christ Jesus for you."
1 Thessalonians 5:16-18 (NKJV)

Copy Memory Verse

_____

_____

_____

_____

Bible Lesson

2 Chronicles 7:14 (NKJV) says, "If My people who are called by My name will <u>humble</u> themselves, and pray and seek My face, and turn from their wicked ways, then will I hear from Heaven, and will forgive their sin and heal their land." When you <u>humble</u> yourself, you say to the Lord that He is greater than you. You show God that you want what He has instead of your own way. When you pray and seek God with a humble heart, God is listening. God makes a promise in this verse. He says that when you pray and turn from your wicked ways (repent of your sin), He will bring forgiveness and healing. God, the Father, is always listening. He loves it when you go to Him in prayer. He loves to fellowship with you. You can talk to Him anytime!

New Words

ceasing

humble

_____

_____

_____

_____

_____

Draw What You Learned

Questions

1. What does it mean to <u>humble</u> yourself?

_____

_____

2. Who is listening to you when you pray?

_____

_____

3. What will God bring when you pray and repent?

_____

_____

4. When can you talk to God?

_____

_____

Closing Prayer

Father, I know that I can talk with you anytime. You are always listening. You love when I spend time with you! Thank you for Your promises. They are always true. In Jesus name, amen.

Holy Spirit comforts_____.

Growing in Christ

Opening Prayer

Weekly Memory Verse

"Rejoice always, 17 pray without <u>ceasing</u>, 18 in everything give thanks; for this is the will of God in Christ Jesus for you."
1 Thessalonians 5:16-18 (NKJV)

Read Aloud Memory Verse

Mark or color each square when completed.

Bible Lesson

Mark 11:24 (NKJV) says, "Therefore I say to you, whatever things you ask when you pray, believe that you receive them, and you will have them." The Bible tells you how important it is to pray and believe. Prayer is how you talk to God. It is important that when you talk to God, you believe in Him. The Bible is full of God's promises. When you read the Word of God you learn about all the promises He has made to you, His child. When you pray, you can talk to God about those promises. Faith is believing even when you don't see it. When you have faith, you can see those promises happen in your life. Faith and prayer go together to see miracles happen.

New Words

ceasing

humble

_____

_____

_____

_____

_____

Draw What You Learned

Questions

1. What is prayer?

_____

_____

2. What is the Bible full of?

_____

_____

3. What can you talk to God about when you pray?

_____

_____

4. What is faith?

_____

_____

Closing Application Prayer

Jesus, I believe all the promises in Your Word. You Word is always true. I am going to remember Your promises when I pray. I know I will see miracles happen. In Your name, amen.

Unit 6 Week 34: Assessment

Opening Prayer

Weekly Memory Verse

_____

_____

_____

_____

Assessment Questions

1. What is one way you can talk to God throughout the day?

_____

_____

2. What happens when you spend time in prayer with God?

_____

_____

3. What three things are God's will for you to do?

_____

_____

4. Who is listening to you when you pray?

_____

_____

5. When can you talk to God?

_____

_____

6. What is prayer?

_____

_____

Closing Prayer

Heavenly Father, this week I have learned about how important it is to spend time with You in prayer. You are always there, and You are always listening. I love You! In Jesus name, amen.

I AM HIS!

_____ is a child of God.

Growing in Christ

Opening Prayer

Weekly Memory Verse

"Make a joyful shout to the Lord, all you lands! 2 Serve the Lord with gladness; Come before His presence with singing." Psalms 100: 1-2 (NKJV)

Copy Memory Verse

_____

_____

_____

_____

Bible Lesson

This week you will read scripture about worshiping God. One way to grow in Christ is to worship the Lord. God is your Creator. He made you. He loves you so much. That is a great reason to make a shout of praise. Then, think about all that Jesus has done for you. His purpose for coming to the earth was to die for every person in the world. He willingly gave Himself as a sacrifice so that you and others could have a relationship with God, the Father. That is a great reason to give God praise. The verse says that all lands should shout for joy. It's not just you that should praise God. Everyone, everywhere, should worship the Lord.

New Words

_____

_____

_____

_____

_____

_____

_____

Draw What You Learned

Questions

1. What is one way to grow in Christ?

_____

_____

2. Why should you praise God?

_____

_____

3. What has Jesus done for you?

_____

_____

4. Who should worship the Lord?

_____

_____

Closing Prayer

Father God, You created me. You love me. You loved me so much that You sent Jesus to die for me. I choose to worship You. I choose to give You praise. In Jesus name, amen.

_____ is valued by God.

Growing in Christ

Opening Prayer

Weekly Memory Verse

"Make a joyful shout to the Lord, all you lands! 2 Serve the Lord with gladness; Come before His presence with singing." Psalms 100: 1-2 (NKJV)

Read Aloud Memory Verse

Mark or color each square when completed.

Bible Lesson

The second verse talks about how you should serve the Lord. Serving can be many things. You can serve the Lord by helping others. You can help your parents, friends, siblings, or even a teacher at church. You can serve the Lord by being kind. Sharing your favorite toy with someone who doesn't have anything to play with is being kind. Making a card to take to a nursing home is being kind. Whatever you choose to do to serve the Lord, the Bible says that you should do it with gladness. You should be happy that you can serve the Lord Who made you and loves you! The Bible says to come into God's presence with singing. God's presence is everywhere, You can sing and worship God anywhere.

New Words

_____

_____

_____

_____

_____

_____

_____

Draw What You Learned

Questions

1. What is one way to serve the Lord?

_____

_____

2. How can you serve the Lord by being kind?

_____

_____

3. How should you serve the Lord?

_____

_____

4. Where is God's presence?

_____

_____

Closing Application Prayer

Father, Your presence is everywhere. I can be close to You, no matter where I am. I choose to serve You with gladness. I want to show others Your love. In Jesus name, amen.

Week 35
Day 173

_____ is loved by God.

Growing in Christ

Opening Prayer

Weekly Memory Verse

"Make a joyful shout to the Lord, all you lands! 2 Serve the Lord with gladness; Come before His presence with singing." Psalms 100: 1-2 (NKJV)

Copy Memory Verse

_____

_____

_____

_____

Bible Lesson

Psalms 100:3 (NKJV) says, "Know that the Lord, He is God; It is He who has made us, and not we ourselves; We are His people and the sheep of His pasture." God is your Creator. He made you. You did not make yourself. All that you are able to do is because God gave you <u>talents</u>, or abilities, to be able to do it. You are God's child. He values you more than anything in the world. When you belong to God it is like you are His sheep and He is your Shepherd. A shepherd always takes care of his sheep. The sheep are not afraid when the shepherd is around. You can praise and worship God and never fear because He is always taking care of you.

New Words

talents

_____

_____

_____

_____

_____

_____

Draw What You Learned

Questions

1. Who is your Creator?

_____

_____

2. What are talents?

_____

_____

3. What is God like?

_____

_____

4. What does a shepherd always do for his sheep?

_____

_____

Closing Prayer

I praise you Jesus! You are my Shepherd. You take care of me and watch over me. I am saved because You died for me. I love You Jesus. In Your mighty name, amen.

Week 35
Day 174

Holy Spirit comforts_____.

Growing in Christ

Opening Prayer

"Make a joyful shout to the Lord, all you lands! 2 Serve the Lord with gladness; Come before His <u>presence</u> with singing." Psalms 100: 1-2 (NKJV)

Read Aloud Memory Verse

Mark or color each square when completed.

Bible Lesson

Psalms 100:4 (NKJV) says, "Enter into His gates with thanksgiving, And into His courts with praise. Be thankful to Him, and bless His name." You have read this week about reasons why you should worship or praise the Lord. If there were no other reason, you should worship the Lord because He is God. He is the King of Kings and Lord of Lords. There is no one as powerful as God. You can enter into His presence at church, outside, or even in your bedroom. Whenever you worship God, you should enter into His presence with gladness, praise, and thanksgiving. The verse also reminds you to bless God's name. You can bless God's name by talking about Him with love and worshiping Him.

New Words

talents

_____

_____

_____

_____

_____

_____

_____

Draw What You Learned

Questions

1. Why should you worship the Lord?

_____

_____

2. Where can you enter into God's presence?

_____

_____

3. What three things should you enter into God's presence with?

_____

_____

4. How can you bless God's name?

_____

_____

Closing Application Prayer

Father God, I have so much to be thankful for. You have done so much for me. I bless and praise Your name. I choose to be in Your presence with a thankful heart. In Jesus name, amen.

Unit 6 Week 35: Assessment

Opening Prayer

Weekly Memory Verse

_____

_____

_____

_____

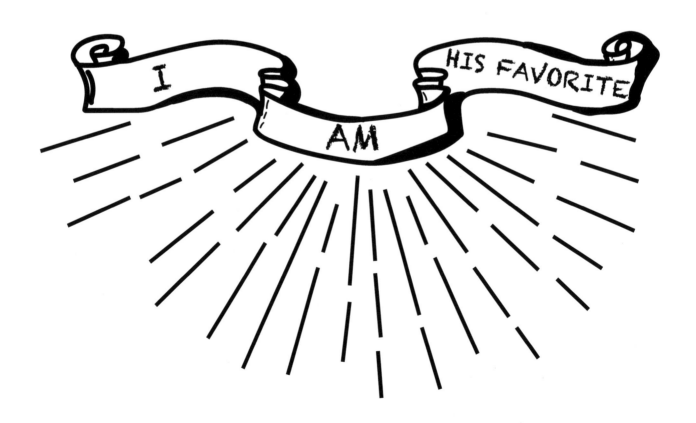

1. Why should you praise God?

_____

_____

2. Who should worship the Lord?

_____

_____

3. What is one way to serve the Lord?

_____

_____

4. How should you serve the Lord?

_____

_____

5. What does a shepherd always do for his sheep?

_____

_____

6. What three things should you enter into God's presence with?

_____

_____

Closing Prayer

Heavenly Father, just like the memory verse says, I choose to come before you with singing and a joyful noise. I will serve you with a glad heart! In Jesus name, amen.

YOU DID GREAT!

_____ is loved by God.

Growing in Christ

Opening Prayer

Weekly Memory Verse

"Hide Your face from my sins, and <u>blot</u> out all my <u>iniquities</u>. 10 Create in me a clean heart, O God, and <u>renew</u> a <u>steadfast</u> spirit within me." Psalm 51: 9-10 (NKJV)

Copy Memory Verse

_____

_____

_____

_____

Bible Lesson

   The <u>Bible</u> calls you to live a holy life. The memory verses this week talks about God forgiving and making you new. King David was the one who spoke these verses. He loved God with all of his heart, but he had done some very bad things. David was talking to God in these verses. He asked God to hide His face from David's sin. David knew that God had seen everything that he had done. David was truly sorry. He asked God to <u>blot</u> out his <u>iniquities</u>. <u>Blot</u> means to completely get rid of and <u>iniquities</u> are sins. David asked God to completely get rid of his sin. When you are truly sorry for what you have done, you ask God to forgive you. You want to be clean and live a holy life.

New Words

blot

iniquities

_____

_____

_____

_____

_____

Draw What You Learned

Questions

1. Who was David talking to in Psalms 51:9-10?

_____

_____

2. What did David ask God to do with his sin?

_____

_____

3. What does blot mean?

_____

_____

4. What do you do when you are truly sorry for your sin?

_____

_____

Closing Prayer

Heavenly Father, I am truly sorry for my sin. I know that You want me to live a holy life. Thank You for helping me to live for You and do what is right. In Jesus name, amen.

Week 36
Day 177

_____ is valued by God.

Growing in Christ

Opening Prayer

"Hide Your face from my sins, and blot out all my <u>iniquities</u>. Create in me a clean heart, O God, and <u>renew</u> a <u>steadfast</u> spirit within me." Psalm 51: 9-10 (NKJV)

Read Aloud Memory Verse

Mark or color each square when completed.

Bible Lesson

David continued his prayer to God by asking God to create a clean heart in him. God was more than willing to forgive David and give him a clean heart. God will forgive you too! You can go to God and repent for anything that you have done. There is no sin that you might do that would keep God from forgiving you. David wanted God to <u>renew</u>, or make new, his spirit. He asked for a <u>steadfast</u> spirit. A <u>steadfast</u> spirit is one that has pure thoughts and wants to live a holy life. God granted that to David. God wants you to repent and desire to live a holy life just like David did.

New Words

blot

iniquities

renew

steadfast

_____

_____

_____

Draw What You Learned

Questions

1. What did David want God to create in him?

_____

_____

2. Who is God willing to forgive?

_____

_____

3. What is a steadfast spirit?

_____

_____

4. What does God want you to do?

_____

_____

Closing Application Prayer

Father, you are so faithful to hear me when I pray. You will forgive me when I ask. I want to live a life that pleases you! I love you! In Jesus name, amen.

Week 36
Day 178

_____ is loved by God.

Growing in Christ

Opening Prayer

Weekly Memory Verse

"Hide Your face from my sins, And blot out all my <u>iniquities</u>. Create in me a clean heart, O God, and <u>renew</u> a <u>steadfast</u> spirit within me." Psalm 51: 9-10 (NKJV)

Copy Memory Verse

_____

_____

_____

_____

Bible Lesson

1 Corinthians 6:19 (NKJV) says, "Or do you not know that your body is the temple of the Holy Spirit who is in you, whom you have from God, and you are not your own." A temple is a place where God lives. This verses says that you are a temple where God lives. When you receive Jesus as your Savior, Holy Spirit comes to live inside of you. This means that you have a responsibility to live a holy life. God is holy. He cannot be where there is sin. God sent Holy Spirit to you to be a Comforter and a Guide. Holy Spirit will help you live a holy life. When you give your life to the Lord, it is no longer your life. You belong to God and you need to live a holy life that follows the example of Jesus.

New Words

blot

iniquities

renew

steadfast

_____

_____

_____

Draw What You Learned

Questions

1. What is a temple?

_____

_____

2. Who lives inside of you?

_____

_____

3. Why did God send Holy Spirit?

_____

_____

4. Who will help you live a holy life?

_____

_____

Closing Prayer

Lord, I know that my body is a temple that You live in because

Jesus is my Savior. My life is not mine anymore, it belongs to you.

I choose to live a holy life. In Jesus name, amen.

Week 36
Day 179

Holy Spirit comforts_____.

Growing in Christ

Opening Prayer

Weekly Memory Verse

"Hide Your face from my sins, And blot out all my <u>iniquities</u>. Create in me a clean heart, O God, and <u>renew</u> a <u>steadfast</u> spirit within me." Psalm 51: 9-10 (NKJV)

Read Aloud Memory Verse

Mark or color each square when completed.

Bible Lesson

1 Corinthians 6:20 (NKJV) says, "For you were bought at a price; therefore glorify God in your body and in your spirit, which are God's." This verse says that you were bought at a price. You were bought at a very great price. That price was the life of Jesus, God's Son. Jesus was beaten, <u>humiliated</u> (made fun of), and killed so that man could come back to God. That is a very high price and Jesus did it all because He loves you so much. In return, the Father asks you to glorify Him in your body and in your spirit because you now belong to Him. This means living a holy life. A holy life is one that lives to please the Lord instead of people.

New Words

blot

iniquities

renew

steadfast

humiliated

_____

_____

Draw What You Learned

Questions

1. Who bought you with a price?

_____

_____

2. What price did Jesus pay for you to be free?

_____

_____

3. Why did Jesus pay that price?

_____

_____

4. What is a holy life?

_____

_____

Closing Application Prayer

Heavenly Father, I choose to live a holy life. I want to please You instead of other people. Thank You, Jesus, for paying the price so I could be free. I love You! In Your Jesus name, amen.

Unit 6 Week 36: Assessment

Opening Prayer

Weekly Memory Verse

_____

_____

_____

_____

1. What do you do when you are truly sorry for your sin?

_____

_____

2. What is a steadfast spirit?

_____

_____

3. What does God want you to do?

_____

_____

4. Why did God send Holy Spirit?

_____

_____

5. What price did Jesus pay for you to be free?

_____

_____

6. What is a holy life?

_____

_____

Closing Prayer

Jesus, thank You for all You have done for me. You have forgiven my sins and You promise to never leave me. I choose to live like You and live a holy life. In Your name, amen.

HE LOVES ME!

Answer Keys

Bible - Unit 4 Week 19 - 20 Answer Key

Unit 4 Week 19 Day 91

1. Twelve disciples who followed Jesus
2. Jesus
3. A broken relationship with God
4. You have salvation

Unit 4 Week 20 Day 96

1. A payment
2. Death
3. They received death
4. Eternal life in Jesus Christ

Unit 4 Week 19 Day 92

1. Repent and turn back to God
2. Ask forgiveness and turn away from sin
3. You become more like Him
4. Brings you peace and strength

Unit 4 Week 20 Day 97

1. To say aloud
2. Jesus
3. Believe in your heart that God raised Jesus from the dead
4. Confess Jesus

Unit 4 Week 19 Day 93

1. Recieve the gift of the Holy Spirit
2. God was sending Holy Spirit
3. Through Holy Spirit
4. Able to do what Jesus did

Unit 4 Week 20 Day 98

1. Passionate
2. Strong emotion
3. A sinner
4. Jesus died for us

Unit 4 Week 19 Day 94

1. A beacon of light to the nations
2. Others can see the way to Jesus
3. To do according to a plan
4. Tell others about Jesus in other nations

Unit 4 Week 20 Day 99

1. Preaching about Jesus
2. Singing and praising God
3. The chains fell off and the doors opened
4. Believe on Jesus

Assessment Questions

1. Jesus
2. Ask forgiveness and turn away from sin
3. You become more like Him
4. God was sending Holy Spirit
5. Able to do what Jesus did
6. A beacon of light to the nations

Assessment Questions

1. Death
2. Eternal life
3. People that are saved
4. Believe in your heart that God raised Jesus from the dead
5. Passionate
6. Jesus died for me

Bible - Unit 4 Week 21 - 22 Answer Key

Unit 4 Week 21 Day 101

1. A new creation
2. When you accept Jesus
3. Their spirits were seperatated from God
4. Your spirit becomes alive

Unit 4 Week 22 Day 106

1. Someone who brings both sides totether
2. Jesus
3. All the people that God created
4. The cool of the evening

Unit 4 Week 21 Day 102

1. Old things
2. All things become new
3. Things you used to do
4. Decide to follow your spirit and not your flesh

Unit 4 Week 22 Day 107

1. With Gratitude
2. Anytime you want
3. Jesus
4. How thankful you are for everything He has done for you

Unit 4 Week 21 Day 103

1. Jesus
2. He took your sin upon Him
3. Righteous
4. He took your sins

Unit 4 Week 22 Day 108

1. Pray for all men
2. With intense passion
3. To speak for someone else
4. Jesus made a way

Unit 4 Week 21 Day 104

1. To meet a bad end
2. Because of sin
3. Accept Jesus and believe in Him
4. Grace

Unit 4 Week 22 Day 109

1. Pray for them
2. To accept
3. His life
4. God loves everyone and does not want to see anyone spend eternity away from Him

Assessment Questions

1. When you accept Jesus
2. A new creation
3. Old things
4. Jesus
5. Jesus took your sin
6. God's grace

Assessment Questions

1. Someone who brings both sides together
2. Jesus
3. With Gratitude
4. To speak for someone else
5. Jesus made a way
6. His life

Bible - Unit 4 Week 23 - 24 Answer Key

Unit 4 Week 23 Day 111

1. Getting what you don't deserve
2. To be seen
3. Grace was manifested in Person
4. Blessings

Unit 4 Week 24 Day 116

1. To tell
2. To God
3. Righteous and true
4. To forgive you

Unit 4 Week 23 Day 112

1. How to live each day
2. Ungodliness and indulgent lifestyles
3. To do what ever you want
4. Give you the ability

Unit 4 Week 24 Day 117

1. Cleanses you from all unrighteousness
2. To make clean
3. Sin
4. Jesus

Unit 4 Week 23 Day 113

1. Jesus
2. We would no longer sin
3. Death and pain
4. Being hurt

Unit 4 Week 24 Day 118

1. Reading the Bible
2. Someone who supports you
3. Jesus
4. Jesus goes to the Father for you

Unit 4 Week 23 Day 114

1. We are like sheep
2. Jesus
3. Watch over them and keep them safe
4. A protector

Unit 4 Week 24 Day 119

1. Jesus
2. From the beginning of the world
3. To make a wrong right
4. Everyone in the whole world

Assessment Questions

1. Getting what you don't deserve
2. Blessings
3. How to live each day
4. We would no longer sin
5. Jesus
6. Watch over them and keep them safe

Assessment Questions

1. To God
2. To forgive you
3. Cleanses you from all unrighteousness
4. Jesus goes to the Father for you
5. From the beginning of the world
6. Everyone in the whole world

Bible - Unit 5 Week 25 - 26 Answer Key

Unit 5 Week 25 Day 121

1. Leave His disciples and go to Heaven
2. His Father's house
3. The glory of God
4. Jesus

Unit 5 Week 26 Day 126

1. To come back from the dead
2. Live with Jesus in Heaven
3. To really want something
4. For things that are above

Unit 5 Week 25 Day 122

1. To make
2. The disciples
3. Heaven
4. No, for me as well

Unit 5 Week 26 Day 127

1. He was on earth
2. Went up into Heaven
3. Put on a throne
4. Power, honor and authority

Unit 5 Week 25 Day 123

1. God created everything
2. People, animals, and plants
3. The sun, moon, stars
4. All that He created

Unit 5 Week 26 Day 128

1. A new heaven and new earth
2. So much pain and destruction
3. When Adam and Eve sinned
4. The things in the past

Unit 5 Week 25 Day 124

1. A prophet
2. Follower of the prophet Elijah
3. A chariot
4. He was taken to Heaven

Unit 5 Week 26 Day 129

1. By the Word of the Lord
2. Where the angels live
3. Power to create
4. With love according to God's word

Assessment Questions

1. His Father's house
2. Jesus
3. Heaven
4. People, animals, and plants
5. Jesus
6. All that He created

Assessment Questions

1. Live with Jesus in Heaven
2. For things that are above
3. Went up into Heaven
4. A new heaven and new earth
5. When Adam and Eve sinned
6. Power to create

Bible - Unit 5 Week 27 - 28 Answer Key

Unit 5 Week 27 Day 131

1. He gave His only begotten Son for me
2. Every person in the world
3. To bring to life
4. He sent His son to die for the whole world

Unit 5 Week 28 Day 136

1. Save Himself
2. Remember him when Jesus entered into His kingdom
3. Heaven
4. He would be with Jesus in Paradise

Unit 5 Week 27 Day 132

1. The world
2. He wanted to spend eternity with you
3. Heaven
4. To die

Unit 5 Week 28 Day 137

1. We will be with Jesus in Paradise
2. No
3. He had done bad things
4. The theif believed that Jesus was the Son of God

Unit 5 Week 27 Day 133

1. On earth
2. Moth and rust
3. Thieves
4. Forever

Unit 5 Week 28 Day 138

1. A tent
2. God made Heaven
3. Forever
4. No one can destroy Heaven

Unit 5 Week 27 Day 134

1. Heaven
2. Because it will last for eternity
3. Do things for the Lord on earth
4. Build treasure in Heaven

Unit 5 Week 28 Day 139

1. A group of people that live in one place
2. Your real home
3. Earth
4. Jesus is our Life-Giver

Assessment Questions

1. He gave His only begotten Son for me
2. Heaven
3. He wanted to spend eternity with you
4. Because it will last for eternity
5. forever
6. Do things for the Lord on earth

Assessment Questions

1. He would be with Jesus in Paradise
2. No
3. The thief believed that Jesus was the Son of God
4. God made Heaven
5. Forever
6. Jesus is our Life-Giver

Bible - Unit 5 Week 29 - 30 Answer Key

Unit 5 Week 29 Day 141

1. His children
2. Noah
3. God would do the impossible
4. Spend time with God

Unit 5 Week 30 Day 146

1. Tells what things look like
2. Twelve gates
3. Made in a shell of a mollusk
4. A pearl

Unit 5 Week 29 Day 142

1. To be embarrassed
2. He loves you so much
3. The city is called Heaven
4. All the people that love Him

Unit 5 Week 30 Day 147

1. Pure gold
2. People
3. A type of glass you can see through
4. Like a crystal

Unit 5 Week 29 Day 143

1. Forever
2. No permanent home for God's children
3. Forever
4. Heaven

Unit 5 Week 30 Day 148

1. A dwelling place of God
2. Go into God's dwelling place
3. God is holy and man sinned
4. Jesus made a way

Unit 5 Week 29 Day 144

1. A new Heaven and new earth
2. Keeps them
3. To expect
4. Righteousness

Unit 5 Week 30 Day 149

1. Death, sorrow, and crying
2. Suffering
3. No
4. All things on earth

Assessment Questions

1. His children
2. Spend time with God
3. Heaven
4. Forever
5. A new Heaven and new earth
6. Righteousness

Assessment Questions

1. Twelve gates
2. A pearl
3. Pure gold
4. People
5. God is holy and man sinned
6. Death, sorrow, and crying

Bible - Unit 6 Week 31 - 32 Answer Key

Unit 6 Week 31 Day 151

1. A follower of someone or something
2. Of all nations
3. Jesus
4. At church, reading the Bible, and talking with Jesus

Unit 6 Week 32 Day 156

1. Holy Spirit
2. Filled with power
3. Through Holy Spirit
4. To know and understand

Unit 6 Week 31 Day 152

1. Get baptized
2. Jesus
3. Jesus' example
4. Helps you live your Christian life

Unit 6 Week 32 Day 157

1. Every part of the world
2. Complete the plan God has for them
3. The good news of what Jesus did
4. So people would know and accept Jesus as their Savior

Unit 6 Week 31 Day 153

1. God the Father
2. Beloved Son, whom I am well pleased
3. John the Baptist
4. God the Father

Unit 6 Week 32 Day 158

1. Those who waited on Him
2. They began to speak in other tongues
3. Spoken word or statement
4. Speaking to the Lord in your Heavenly language

Unit 6 Week 31 Day 154

1. Forty days
2. "Follow me and I will make you fishers of men"
3. Teaching others how to be saved
4. Three years

Unit 6 Week 32 Day 159

1. Holy Spirit
2. God the Father
3. To live with
4. They can not see or know Him

Assessment Questions

1. A follower of someone or something
2. Jesus
3. Be baptized
4. Jesus's name
5. Beloved Son, whom I am well pleased
6. Teaching others how to be saved

Assessment Questions

1. Holy Spirit
2. Filled with Power
3. Every part of the world
4. Those who waited on Him
5. Speaking to the Lord in your Heavenly language
6. Holy Spirit

Bible – Unit 6 Week 33 – 34 Answer Key

Unit 6 Week 33 Day 161

1. The Bible
2. God
3. Men, led by Holy Spirit
4. One way you can grow in Christ

Unit 6 Week 34 Day 166

1. To stop
2. Pray without stopping
3. Thanking God for your meals
4. You will become more like Jesus

Unit 6 Week 33 Day 162

1. Reproofing and correcting
2. Helping to make wrong things right
3. Things that need to be changed in your life
4. How to live a life of righteousness

Unit 6 Week 34 Day 167

1. Pray without ceasing
2. God is with you
3. Rejoice, be thankful, and pray
4. God will never leave you

Unit 6 Week 33 Day 163

1. Make a hole in
2. Alive
3. Reason for doing something
4. The Bible

Unit 6 Week 34 Day 168

1. Say that God is greater than you
2. God is listening
3. Bring forgiveness and healing
4. You can talk anytime to God

Unit 6 Week 33 Day 164

1. Hides God's Word in your heart
2. Reading, meditating, and memorize it
3. Ask Holy Spirit
4. You stay out of trouble

Unit 6 Week 34 Day 169

1. How you talk to God
2. Full of promises
3. Talk to God about His promises
4. Believing even when you don't see it

Assessment Questions

1. The Bible
2. God
3. Reproofing and correcting
4. Alive
5. Reading, meditating, and memorize it
6. You stay out of trouble

Assessment Questions

1. Thanking God for your meals
2. You will become more like Jesus
3. Rejoice, be thankful, and pray
4. God is listening
5. You can talk to God anytime
6. How you talk to God

Bible - Unit 6 Week 35 - 36 Answer Key

Unit 6 Week 35 Day 171

1. Worship the Lord
2. God is our creator
3. Gave Himself as a sacrifice
4. Everyone

Unit 6 Week 36 Day 176

1. God
2. Hide His face from David's sins
3. Completely get rid of
4. Ask God to forgive you

Unit 6 Week 35 Day 172

1. By helping others
2. Make a card for the Nursing home
3. Do it with gladness
4. Everywhere

Unit 6 Week 36 Day 177

1. A clean heart
2. He will forgive me
3. Pure thoughts and wants to live a Holy life
4. Repent and live a Holy life

Unit 6 Week 35 Day 173

1. God is your Creator
2. Abilities
3. He is your Shepherd
4. Takes care of His sheep

Unit 6 Week 36 Day 178

1. Your body is a temple
2. God lives inside of you
3. To be a Comforter and a Guide
4. Holy Spirit

Unit 6 Week 35 Day 174

1. He is God
2. Church, outside, or in your bedroom
3. Gladness, praise, and thanksgiving
4. Talking about Him and worshiping Him

Unit 6 Week 36 Day 179

1. God bought you
2. His life
3. Man could come back to God
4. Glorify Him in your body and spirit

Assessment Questions

1. God created us
2. Everyone
3. By helping others
4. Talking about Him and worshiping Him
5. Takes car of His sheep
6. Gladness, praise and thanksgiving

Assessment Questions

1. Repent
2. Pure thoughts and wants to live a Holy life
3. Repent and live a Holy life
4. To be a Comforter and a Guide
5. His life
6. Glorify Him in your body and spirit